MAGNUS MAGNUSSON KBE, broadcaster and writer, is chairman of Scottish Natural Heritage, the government's advisory body on environmental issues, which owns and manages the island of Rum as a National Nature Reserve. A lover of the countryside all his life, he was President of the Royal Society for the Protection of Birds (1985-89), and was chairman of the Nature Conservancy Council for Scotland (1991-92) before its merger with the Countryside Commission for Scotland to form SNH in 1992.

Known to millions as the television quizmaster of *Mastermind* throughout its highly acclaimed 25-year run, he also presented *Tonight, Chronicle* and *Living Legends.* He has written several books on archaeology and history (he was awarded the Medlicott Medal of the Historical Association in 1989), on his native Iceland (including *Iceland Saga* and *Vikings!)* and on his adopted country of Scotland (including *Treasures of Scotland* and *The Nature of Scotland).* He has also translated many of the classical Icelandic Sagas, and some modern novels by the Icelandic Nobel Prize-winner, Halldór Laxness.

In recognition of his many services to Scotland he was awarded an honorary knighthood (KBE) in 1989. He is also a Knight Commander of the Icelandic Order of the Falcon (1986).

D0265430

Rum: Nature's Island

MAGNUS MAGNUSSON

Luath Press Limited

THE ROYAL MILE · EDINBURGH
www.luath.co.uk

First Edition 1997

Details of titles currently available
from Luath are set out on the final
pages of this book.

The paper in this book is acid-free,
neutral-sized and recyclable.
It is made from low chlorine pulps
produced in a low energy and emission
manner from sustainable forests.
Printed and bound by
The Cromwell Press, Melksham

Typeset in 9½ point Sabon by
RedLetter Ltd., Edinburgh

Contents

PART TWO: THE PRESENT

General map of Rum

Preface

FOR FORTY YEARS NOW, the island of Rum in the Inner Hebrides has been in public ownership and managed as a National Nature Reserve. It is a marvellous national asset, owned and administered by Scottish Natural Heritage on behalf of the people of Scotland. This book tells the story of Rum, from earliest geological time to the present day.

It used to be called 'Rhum', not Rum; indeed, until relatively recently it was recorded by the Ordnance Survey as 'Rhum'. No one now knows what its original name was. The earliest written record is in the seventh century Annals of Ulster, where the name was written as 'Ruiminn'. There have been suggestions that when the Norsemen arrived in western waters they called the island *Rømøy*, meaning 'Roomy Island', but there is no documentary evidence to support this. A simple shortening of 'Ruiminn' to Rum seems more likely

As for the 'Rhum' spelling – that was a spurious late Victorian whim. Perhaps 'Rum' was felt to be rather a plebeian name for a sporting estate, or that it needed embroidery with some phoney Celticism by adding an 'h', on the ground that all Gaelic words seemed to contain an 'h' in every second syllable. In fact, Gaelic has no words beginning 'Rh-'. Nonetheless, the last private owner of Rum, Sir George Bullough, was most insistent on spelling it 'Rhum' (perhaps because his wife, Monica, was a lifelong teetotaller!). When the island was 'inherited' by Scottish Natural Heritage in 1992, the old spelling was revived to bring it back into line with Gaelic usage, although it should more accurately be shown as 'Rùm' and pronounced 'Room'.

The spellings of all the other Gaelic place-names in this book have been standardised in line with a comprehensive review undertaken on behalf of Scottish Natural Heritage in 1996 by Peadar Morgan of CLI (Comunn an Luchd-Ionnsachaidh), who regularised the orthography and established a correct form for each of the island's place-names.

This book is a celebration of the 40 years of public ownership of Rum. To that end it tries to place the island's story into the context of its geological origins and its human inhabitants and owners down the centuries. I can claim little personal credit for it – it is essentially a compilation of the work of others, a formidable array of experts who have laboured for years on the many fascinating aspects of Rum: its history, its natural history, its archaeology, all its life and earth sciences, in fact. They have generously allowed me to make unrestricted use of their published and unpublished endeavours.

I owe a huge debt of gratitude to them all, and their names are duly listed in the Acknowledgements and Sources. Suffice it here to highlight the major contributions, both general and particular, made by Martin Ball, John Baxter, John Morton Boyd, Tim Clutton-Brock, Roger Crofts, Martin Curry, Clive Hollingworth, Ben Leyshon, John Love, Peter Mackay, Alan McKirdy, George Randall, Michael Scott, Chris Smout, Chris Sydes, Des Thompson, Rob Threadgould, Michael B Usher, John Walters, Jeff Watson, Caroline Wickham-Jones and Peter Wormell, with special thanks to Iain Sarjeant for his line-drawings. I am also grateful to Elaine Dunlop, SNH Publications Manager, for her help with the illustrations, to Mary McNab, SNH Secretariat, for her sterling preliminary work on the Index, and to my secretary, Marion Whitelaw, for much patient work in tracking down contacts and checking vital facts and figures.

Magnus Magnusson KBE
August, 1997

Introduction

THE INTRODUCTION to any book on Rum, even by the Chief Executive of the body which owns the island, cannot be written in the dispassionate language of a management plan. For anyone who has visited Rum there is a sense of awe at the grandeur of the landscape, a sense of expectation of the wildlife to be seen and heard, a sense of curiosity about the secrets still locked in its rocks and landforms, a sense of sorrow at the impoverishment of the island and of its indigenous inhabitants before their unseemly clearance to Canada, and a sense of incredulity at the Edwardian transformation of it.

Driving through the native oakwoods of south Morar and Arisaig does not prepare one for the first sight of the Small Isles as one reaches the coast at Arisaig village. On a clear day the sentinel-like Sgurr of Eigg and the jagged peaks of the Rum Cuillin dominate the seascape and dwarf the rest of these islands; on a less clear day the helm clouds on the Rum Cuillin could easily be mistaken for the effusion from the great volcano which dominated the landscape some 60 million years ago. Mystery and allusions to past times abound. Passing through the Sound of Rum, with Eigg to starboard and Rum to port, the eastern flank of the Rum Cuillin towers above you and the coast looks severe and inhospitable. Turning into the haven of Loch Scresort, however, one enters another world: tree-clad slopes (the result of inspired initiatives by former owners) and the turrets of an incongruous castle built of alien stone.

As a geomorphologist by training, for me the real Rum is found in the very heart of the island. Standing on the Cuillin ridge one can see the island in its proper setting, with the Long Island hazy to the west and the other volcanic remnants looming to the north (the Skye Cuillin) and south (Ardnamurchan and Ben More, Mull). Close at hand are the magnificent exposures of banded stone which have stimulated the interest of so many geologists. On the western hills one marvels at the strange landforms for which Rum is rightly renowned.

Harris is an extraordinarily evocative place: a raised beach created by ancient waves which shaped large pebbles and dumped them high above the shore; the vestiges of the community of forty households of two centuries ago, eking out a subsistence living from the land; the vivid remains of one of the most extensive series of 'lazybeds' in Scotland; and the utter incongruity, in the setting of this abandoned crofting township, of the burial mausoleum of the Bulloughs, owners of the island for a mere 70 years. It symbolises the island's long cultural history: the first recorded settlement in Scotland (at Kinloch), the changes of ownership, the development of crofting and its clearance in favour of sheep and then

sport, and ultimately its acquisition by a Government nature conservation agency.

Similarly, the woodlands at the head of Kilmory Glen are sympto-
matic of a new, or at least a revived, world of humid West Coast woodland, with native trees and an abundant woodland flora and fauna.
Walking through them now is an unforgettable experience.

The combination of cultural and natural history is one which
has attracted visitors for years, despite the island's former reputation
of being 'the Forbidden Isle'. Those who come to this Hebridean
gem, whether scientists, climbers or tourists, seldom fail to come again,
and again.

But despite all the efforts of our colleagues over the past 40 years,
the ecology of the island is not what it should be: the gem is tarnished
and has had some bits knocked off. On Rum we see the effects of millennia of misuse: the removal of trees and shrubs for fuel and for other
domestic uses; the burning of the vegetation to increase its palatability
(only to find that it was done far too frequently and probably too harsh-
ly, so that it left the soil impoverished); the effects of grazing and browsing by sheep, goats and deer to a point well beyond the carrying capacity of the land, and certainly to the detriment of the islanders who
depended upon its produce. The gradually worsening climate over the
last few millennia, with increased precipitation and lower temperatures,
has certainly exacerbated the damage, further reducing the quality of
the soils and the carrying capacity of the land.

No less significant for Scottish Natural Heritage as the owners of
Rum is the poor state of the properties which survive from the Bullough
era, particularly Kinloch Castle itself (see CHAPTER 6). Looking after
historic buildings is no part of our natural heritage remit. Having failed
to transfer these onerous responsibilities to a more appropriate guardian
(see CHAPTER 16), we have been able only to keep the castle wind-and
-water-tight; we have not yet been able to make any real progress
towards making lasting improvements for the future.

Our legacy

This book rightly salutes the pioneers who made possible the acquisition of Rum, like Max Nicholson (then Director-General of the Nature
Conservancy), John Arbuthnott (now the Viscount of Arbuthnott, who
was the NC's Land Agent for Scotland), and the late Joe Eggeling, the
Nature Conservancy's Conservation Officer (Scotland). It pays merited
tribute, too, to the work of those who saw to the early implementation
of the vision for Rum: Peter Wormell, the first Warden/Naturalist, and
the late George McNaughton, the first Warden and, later, Chief Warden (CHAPTER 7).

The responsibility placed on the Nature Conservancy, the first of

SNH's predecessor bodies, was immense. The early Management Plans outline the primary objectives of 'research aimed at recreating the natural characteristics of a Hebridean island' (1960-64) and 'to bring the island to a higher level of biological production than at present and one that can be sustained naturally by the environment' (1965-69). The Plan for 1970-74 specified the objectives much more closely, gave scientific research a lower priority and heralded the importance of grazing by both domestic and native animals. The 1977-82 Plan, by the newly established Nature Conservancy Council (NCC), implied a broadening of the objectives to include education and public access.

The final revision of the management objectives for the Reserve by the Nature Conservancy Council for the period 1987/96 again summarised the guiding principles of restoration through management and manipulation of nature:

> to allow natural development of the island ecosystem under the minimum management necessary to maintain and enhance nature conservation interests, the latter by habitat and species manipulation and restoration, to encourage use of the reserve by outside organisations for research (both applied and strategic) and for education, and to maintain the current level of public access.

Over the past 40 years some very significant achievements have been made:

· The successful establishment of 1050 hectares of woodland through the planting of more than a million trees, the vast majority grown in the tree nursery and latterly using seed from Rum sources (CHAPTER 8);
· the reintroduction of the white-tailed (sea) eagle (CHAPTER 10);
· the recording of the flora and fauna so that Rum is the best documented of all of the islands (CHAPTER 9);
· the successful undertaking of critical research on the volcanic complex (CHAPTER 1) and on the biology of red deer (CHAPTER 11);
· the encouragement of visitors both to learn about and enjoy the island (CHAPTER 15).

So the gem is on the road to recovery, and anyone arriving in Loch Scresort or walking the Heritage Trail on the north side of Kinloch Glen (CHAPTER 15) can see the beginnings of the transformation. Not only is the growth of trees and the arrival of woodland ground cover evident but also the birds and insects characteristic of woodlands have arrived.

SNH's vision

SNH's vision for Rum is in one sense simple: to improve the biological productivity and biological diversity of the island so that it contains the whole range of habitats and species which would naturally occur at the present time on a humid West Coast Hebridean island. That is a legitimate vision in its own right; and it will result in an increase in the carrying capacity of the island, so that we and our successors will be able to make choices about the level and type of human activity on Rum without ever again undermining its natural capacity. To achieve this vision is very challenging and very resource-intensive; it will take many decades, and require input from many others. The key words are the three Ps: productiveness, protection and people.

Productiveness

Our predecessors have demonstrated that the island's biological productivity and diversity can be increased with the planting of trees to develop a woodland ecosystem. We have identified other areas where the remnants of a woodland flora are still present; this will help to inform our decisions on where to direct our future efforts at regeneration through planting, which in time will become self-sustaining. However, we are not concerned solely with woodland environments. Rum is of European significance for its wet heaths and its high montane habitats; we shall consider what is required in order to maintain and, where possible, improve their status.

One thing is abundantly clear: grazing and browsing pressure must be reduced. It is our intention to reduce progressively the number of red deer, probably by a half. This reduction will not undermine opportunities for studying the impact of herbivores on the habitats, nor for drawing out lessons from current research for application elsewhere in Scotland.

We are also considering increasing the size of our fold of Highland cattle. Their reintroduction in 1971 has been entirely positive in terms of habitat management of the herb-rich grasses of the Harris machair and in Kilmory Glen. With increased numbers we shall be able to ensure greater continuity of grazing in these areas and at other sites, such as Guirdil and Kilmory.

Rum's herd of some 200 wild goats is a rather different issue. Goats are undoubtedly voracious browsers and can get to places, especially rocky ledges, which no other large herbivore can reach. SNH has to determine the balance between their impact on vegetation generation and the maintenance of semi-native animal communities.

With the progressive reduction in grazing pressure we shall start removing the fencing around the plantation enclosures. We believe that on Rum we should be able to demonstrate habitat regeneration through grazing management without the use of fencing.

Protection

SNH sees 'protection' as a positive concept. To us, protection means that the way in which the island is managed and used not only does not damage its natural interests but also, wherever possible, enhances their chances of development and the benefits they can bring to people. On Rum, as the chapters which follow admirably demonstrate, we have features of international and European significance, foremost among them being the Tertiary volcanic rocks of the main Rum Cuillin complex and of the western area, the periglacial landforms of the western hills, and the plants and birds of the wet heaths and the high hills. This collection of interests is protected through the island being designated as an SSSI for biological and geological reasons, as a Special Protection Area under the Birds Directive for its numbers of nesting seabirds (most notably the Manx shearwater populations and the breeding red-throated divers), and potentially as a Special Area of Conservation under the EU Habitats and Species Directive (most notably for its extensive Atlantic wet heath and a range of sub-montane and sub-maritime heaths and grasslands).

But perhaps the best way of indicating the importance of the island is to log its wildlife: 590 higher plant species, 374 mosses and liverworts, 352 lichens, 889 fungi, 202 birds, 12 other vertebrates, 64 crustaceans, 72 spiders and 2,158 insects of 17 orders have all been recorded in published checklists. All of these factors make protection of the natural heritage of Rum an imperative. Truly Rum is 'Nature's Island'; but it will never again become 'the Forbidden Isle'.

People

We shall continue to encourage people to come to the island to study, to apply new thinking and new theories to what they observe and measure on Rum, to develop new ways of managing land with both people and the environment as beneficiaries. We want people to be able to learn from what the experts are discovering and thereby to become more knowledgeable themselves. We want people to enjoy to the full the experience of Rum: its natural and human history, its landscapes and its wildlife.

People should visit Rum to enjoy and to reflect, to walk and to climb, to paint and to photograph, to study and to research, to learn and to educate; but all these activities and many others must be compatible with the protection of nature and the achievement of greater biological productivity. The island must be managed within an ethic of environmental sustainability. This means that the vital assets of Rum – its rocks, soils, plants, animals and scenery – should be protected now so that they can continue to be used, studied and enjoyed by future generations in perpetuity. People should therefore look after Rum.

And people should live on Rum. For many years, nearly all the residents of Rum have been the employees, and their families, of SNH and its predecessor bodies. It is our intention to continue to have staff based permanently on Rum. We certainly do not intend to become an absentee landowner; but we would like the human community of Rum to be enabled to develop on its own. We recognise that many people see Rum, along with the other Hebridean islands and the adjacent mainland, as 'the lost land' whose indigenous population was sent overseas against its will. We anticipate that one of the outcomes of increasing the productivity of the land will be to create opportunities for others who are not in SNH's employment to live and work on the island, and also for staff to be able to stay on and enjoy their retirement there (see CHAPTER 16).

We recognise that we must find a means of securing the cultural heritage of the island, especially Kinloch Castle and its contents. While this is not the statutory purpose of SNH, we recognise a responsibility to establish mechanisms which will protect that heritage, make it available for research and study, and make it available for the accommodation and enjoyment of visitors. We must also ensure that it is actively used, as we intend Rum to be a living island and not a museum.

Finally, we want the island and its people to develop closer relations with the other Small Isles, in step with the exciting developments on Eigg now that it is in community ownership. It is not our intention to compete with or mimic the activities on Canna, Muck and Eigg; but together we can promote new Hebridean initiatives which demonstrate that people and the environment can be interdependent for the benefits of both in the longer term.

Roger Crofts,
Chief Executive, Scottish Natural Heritage

CHAPTER I

In the Beginning

Rocks of ages

THE ISLAND OF RUM is a volcano which died about 60 million years ago. That is an over-simplified way of putting it, but the ruin of that ancient volcano is what has given the island its unmistakably dominant profile among the Small Isles of the Inner Hebrides. The underlying story of Rum began long before the death of the volcano, however – some three billion years ago, in fact – and involves a remarkable journey across the face of the Earth.

For most of its life, much of what we now call Rum formed part of one of the many differently-sized plates which move slowly around the globe, part of a continent known to geologists as *Laurentia;* like many parts of the Highlands and Islands west of the major divide of the Moine Thrust, the 'basement' rocks of Rum are the hard crystalline Lewisian gneisses and associated rocks, formed almost 3 billion years ago. Some 800 million years ago it was lying in the centre of another supercontinent 30 degrees south of the present position of the equator. Over the

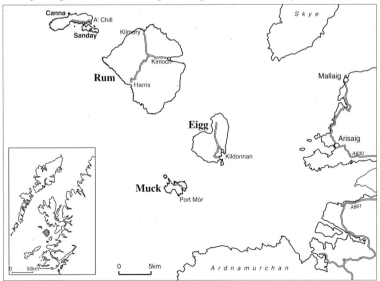

The 'Parish of the Small Isles'

I

aeons of time it wandered the southern hemisphere before drifting north across the equator. By the time it had reached its present position, 60 million years or so ago, the huge expanse which is now the North Atlantic Ocean was merely a narrow strait between present-day Greenland and the continent of Europe.

During its journey Rum experienced many different climates, and many different rocks were deposited. Perhaps the most significant of these periods was that time about 800 million years ago, when Rum formed part of a huge flood-plain crossed by wide shallow rivers. It was in this period that the ancient red-brown pebbly sandstone, named Torridonian after the Torridon area of the mainland, and other sedimentary rocks (notably shales), were formed. These rocks, some 4,500 metres in thickness, now comprise the low hills of the northern part of the island, typified by many benches separated by small escarpments; they also outcrop along the eastern and southern edges of the Cuillin.

There is then a huge gap in the geological story. With the exception of the terrestrial orange-brown sandstones of Monadh Dubh, and small fragments of the sedimentary rocks (seen at Allt nam Bà) laid down when much of Scotland was submerged under the sea, there is little in the visible rocks of Rum to tell us what was happening.

Volcano

A three-million-year volcanic period, some 60 million years ago, was crucial to the formation of present-day Rum. At that time this part of Scotland was an upland area, more than 500 metres high, covered with sub-tropical forests. It was a time of violent volcanic activity as the Earth's crust began to stretch and the North Atlantic Ocean began to develop. All along the western seaboard of Scotland a string of volcanoes began to erupt – Arran, Mull, Ardnamurchan, Skye, St Kilda and Rum, which was one of the first.

The thinning and rifting of the Earth's crust reduced the pressure on the solid rocks below and caused parts of them to melt, so that the liquid rock (magma) rose from depths as great as 100 km along cracks and vents in the crust towards the Earth's surface. Some of the magma poured across the landscape as lava; examples of lava pre-dating the development of the Rum volcano, representing part of the Eigg and Muck lavafields, can be seen in the Allt nam Bà area.

Other magma cooled and solidified in the vents, and was exposed millions of years later as 'dykes' and 'sills', seen now especially in the northern part of Rum along the coast between Kilmory and Guirdil, and along the south-west coast between A' Bhrìdeanach and Harris.

Three stages of the volcanic period have been detected on Rum, and each has made a distinctive contribution to the present landscape.

In the **first stage** in the development of the Rum volcano, granitic

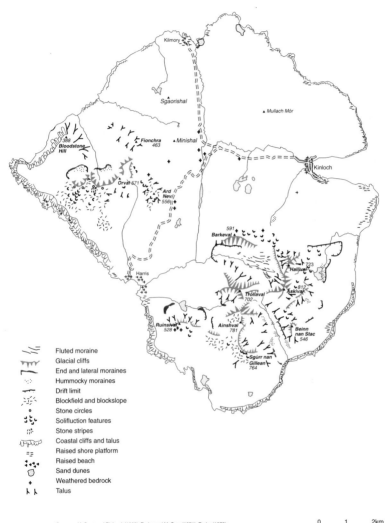

Kilmory

Sgaorishal

▲ Mullach Mòr

388
Bloodstone
Hill

Fionchra
463

▲ Minishal

Kinloch

Orval 671

Ard
Nev
556

591
Barkeval ▲

Harris

Hallival
123

Askival
812

Trollaval
702

Ruinsival
528

Ainshval
781

Beinn
nan Stac
546

Sgùrr nan
Gillean
764

⌇⟍	Fluted moraine
⊤⊤⊤	Glacial cliffs
⌐	End and lateral moraines
⊢	Drift limit
⸬⸓	Blockfield and blockslope
°	Stone circles
⸱⸵	Solifluction features
⸲⸲	Stone stripes
⟨⟩⟩	Coastal cliffs and talus
=⸗	Raised shore platform
⸱⸱⸱	Raised beach
○	Sand dunes
+	Weathered bedrock
⅄ ⅄	Talus

Sources: McCann and Richards(1969): Ryder and McCann(1971): Ryder (1975)
Ballantyne and Wain Hobson (1980): Ballantyne (1984).

0   1   2km

Rum: principal landforms

magmas welled up to make the land surface bulge into a dome shape, some 2,000 metres high. Subsequent reduction of magma pressure caused the dome to collapse, creating a huge central depression known as a caldera. This process, which caused a subsidence of some 2,000 metres, set off paroxysms of explosions and eruptions of hot ash and gas.

The escape of gases, and the catastrophic collapse of the caldera walls, generated rocks known as breccias. Made up of massive blocks, these now form the northern rim of the Rum Cuillin, including Coire Dubh, and much of the Ainshval and Sgùrr nan Gillean hills in the South Cuillin. The ash flows (perhaps similar in nature to those formed in more recent times on the island of Montserrat) settled in the caldera.

The intrusion of granitic bodies followed. They now form the western surface of Rum south of Fionchra and Bloodstone Hill. On Ard Nev the older Lewisian gneiss rocks are seen *over* the younger volcanic rocks, testifying that the latter cooled below the surface. The final episode of this stage was renewed uplift (of around 2,000 metres), which explains the position of rocks within the Main Ring Zone at Allt nam Bà. The boundary of this movement is a fault, known as the Main Ring Fault, encircling the Rum Cuillin.

The **second stage** in the volcano's development was the formation of the spectacular layers of rocks which now form the heart of the Rum Cuillin and are especially prominent on Hallival and Askival. Sixteen alternating layers, each tens of metres thick, interleaved with thinner layers of only a few centimetres, created a remarkable rock sequence some 700 metres thick; the minerals in the rock were probably deposited by gravity, rather like sediments descending on to the floor of a lake. The very particular type found in the south-west, with a coral-like structure of a crystal called olivine, has been termed 'harrisite' after the old crofting township on Rum.

Taken together, all these activities created a broad and shallow-sided volcano (what geologists call a 'shield volcano') which is thought to have been 100 km wide and 2,000m high.

The remnants of the **final stage** of volcanic activity are best seen on the western hills. Here we find the only example in Britain (from this geological era) where the lavas are obviously younger than the central volcano; these are seen on Bloodstone Hill, Fionchra and Orval, where there are four lava flows which probably originated somewhere to the west of Rum. In the sub-tropical climate (as seen from soil horizons in some of the sedimentary rocks of the period) the main volcano lost its top and was quickly eroded by water. The rivers were strong enough to erode channels in the volcanic rocks to the west of the Cuillin, and in those valleys were dumped the rocks from the volcano itself. Here we find the 'puddingstone' rocks (rounded boulders set in sands:

conglomerate) in the river valleys, and sandstones and finer-grained rock in the lochs.

The Rum complex of igneous rocks provides one of the best outdoor laboratories in the world for the study of basaltic volcanoes and the processes which form them.

From fire to ice

Over the next 50 million years after the Rum volcano had exhausted itself, its appearance underwent a transformation. In the warm, humid, subtropical climate the processes of erosion stripped away the top of the volcano and exposed its now cold, solid innards. In all, about a kilometre-depth of volcanic rock was removed. It was probably during this period that the volcanic rocks were also stripped from the northern part of the island to reveal the underlying Torridonian sandstone.

The next phase of Rum's history was the Ice Ages. Over the last two million years it is likely that Rum was covered with ice sheets from the mainland on a number of occasions. It also experienced the development of local ice-caps and associated mountain glaciers. In between these ice periods there were periods of warmer climate. As far as we can tell, the erosional landforms reflect the cumulative effects of many glaciations, but the deposits we see today relate only to the last cold period, from about 115,000–10,000 years ago: they represent ice-sheet glaciation, mountain glaciation, higher sea levels than at present, and cold-climate frost weathering.

The ice sheet and its component glacier tongues moved across Rum from the mainland in a westerly and north-westerly direction. They exploited the softer rocks and the fault lines to deepen the main glens, especially Kilmory and Kinloch Glens; they scoured the bedrock, smoothing it and polishing it in places and leaving the landscape strewn with debris, including boulders of rock not found elsewhere on Rum. The effects of the erosion of the rocks by ice is best seen in the Cuillin: the grinding out of large hollows at the head of Glen Harris and Glen Dibidil, and the formation of small hollows or corries such as Coire nan Grunnd on Hallival and Coire Dubh on Barkeval. Deposits from the glaciers and ice caps cover much of the lower ground.

A final period of glacier activity occurred around 11,000 years ago – the time of the Loch Lomond Stadial and Re-advance (so named because the deposits it left were first identified at Loch Lomond). At this stage Rum probably had its own glaciers in the corries of the Cuillin and the western hills of Orval and Sròn an t-Saighdeir. This glacial period lasted for about a millennium and its effects are recognisable on the ground in the form of an outer ridge of moraines with more irregular hummocky moraines inside them, for instance in the corries of Sròn an t-Saighdeir and Orval, at the head of Glen Harris and in Coire nan Grunnd.

At the same time, a series of landforms representing cold-climate (periglacial) frost weathering was formed. Indeed, the western hills of Rum contain some of the most spectacular periglacial forms in the Inner Hebrides. Here we find the classic 'patterned' ground characteristic of periglacial areas, with the rock debris of various sizes sorted into regular shapes such as lobes, circles and 'stripes'. Some of the periglacial landforms are still active.

The continued freezing and thawing in the cooler months, the steepness of the slopes and, particularly, the finer-grained material which makes it more susceptible to frost action, provide the perfect conditions for geomorphological activity today. Blocks of rock move slowly down the slopes until they build up so much soil and vegetation in front of them that they come to a halt; soil and vegetation also creep down the slopes in an irregular fashion and form terraces with banks of turf at their outer margin, while winds scour off the surface material. Not all the forms we see on the slopes today are created by frost action. In its exposed position, Rum has also a great deal of wind erosion, especially on exposed cols; the scars can best be seen on Ruinsival and between Barkeval and Hallival.

During the many periods of glaciation the western seaboard was pressed down under the enormous weight of the ice, and the sea-level at times was higher relative to the land than it is today. On Rum, shorelines were cut and beaches were deposited by wave action at different levels. Several such levels are found: a rock platform at about 20 metres above sea-level shows signs of having been scratched by ice action, and was possibly formed before the last glaciation at a time when the ice lay to the east of Rum; other shorelines formed as the last ice sheet melted (15–14,000 years ago) and also after the last Ice Age, about 7-6,000 years ago. It was at the latter time that the material which forms the present beaches on the island, including those at Loch Scresort and at Kilmory, was brought to the coast. At Kilmory the sand was subsequently fashioned by wind action into dunes and machairs, and at Harris very large shingle bars were thrown up by the waves.

The island today

That is the story of how Rum came about: an island distinctively diamond-shaped, measuring about 13 km (8 miles) between the farthest points – some 10,700 ha (26,500 acres) in all. It is much the largest of the group of four islands which make up the romantically-named 'Parish of the Small Isles': Rum, Eigg, Canna and Muck.

The resultant topography of Rum can be divided roughly into three broad areas, based on the underlying geology:

much of the **north** and **east** of the island consists of terraced uplands of red-brown sandstones, dotted with shallow lochs and lochans;

the **south-west** is identified by the rounded, crystalline-rock hills of Orval (571m, 1,873ft), Ard Nev (556m, 1,824ft) and Sròn an t-Saighdeir (520m, 1,706ft), and the most striking of the island's sea-cliffs, stretching from the western headland of A' Bhrìdeanach southwards to Harris Bay. It is in this part of the island that the finest periglacial landforms and raised shorelines are found;

the **south-east** block (almost half the island) features the mountain massif to the south of Kinloch Glen containing the 'Rum Cuillin', penetrated by the deep valleys of Glen Dibidil, Glen Harris and Fiachanais. It represents the eroded remains of an ancient volcano which has been subjected to intensive glacial erosion. Here are the five highest mountains of Rum: Hallival (723m, 2,372ft) and Askival (the highest at 812m, 2,664ft) perched at the ends of a lofty knife-edge ridge, with Trollaval (702m, 2,303ft), Ainshval (781m, 2,562ft) and Sgùrr nan Gillean (764m, 2,507ft) rimming the wild valley of Fiachanais.

Three rivers radiate out from Long Loch in the centre of the island (although 'rivers' is a euphemism here for fair-sized streams):

the **Kilmory River** runs north, following the Long Loch fault-line and meandering in the lower reaches through a wide, marshy grazing flat, before cutting through the machair and entering the sandy expanse of Kilmory Bay;

the **Kinloch River** has its sources both north and south of Kinloch Glen. The main stream starts off northwards but soon turns sharply east, flowing down the south side of Kinloch Glen through moorland and peat bogs; it is joined by a tributary which issues out of Loch Bealach MhicNèill over an impressive waterfall there. The river flows over a flat floor of bog before burbling past the agricultural land at Kinloch to the low-tide silt of Loch Scresort;

the **Abhainn Sgathaig** runs south before being joined by the little Abhainn Rangail running west from the heart of the Cuillin in Glen Harris.

Such is Rum today – an endlessly fascinating and physically complex landscape fashioned by geology, a landscape born of fire but shaped by ice, frost, wind and sea. Its landforms epitomise and illuminate the fundamental forces which have shaped the surface of our planet. For earth scientists, both lay and learned, Rum is a paradise.

CHAPTER 2

The Coming of Man

Mesolithic findings

WITH THE END OF THE ICE AGE the climate in Scotland warmed rapidly. Pollen grains of plants on Rum, together with sediments preserved in peat bogs and on the floors of lochs, show that the spread of pioneer vegetation communities (various heathland plants like crowberry and juniper shrub) was followed by the development of woodland comprising birch, hazel, willow and alder. At the same time the root systems of the plants began to develop soils in the humid climate. The improved climatic conditions throughout Scotland provided the habitats to support a range of new animals like the mammoth and the woolly rhinoceros (but not necessarily on Rum). These did not survive in Scotland for long, but others did – elk, wild cattle, red deer, wild horse, wolf, lynx, beaver, bear and smaller mammals, alongside a range of birds, fish, shellfish and sea mammals.

Not long afterwards, according to archaeologist Caroline Wickham-Jones (*Scotland's First Settlers*, 1994),

> a new animal arrived, one that was to have a lasting effect on the land: *Homo sapiens sapiens,* who hunted, cleared and gathered in the quest for food and shelter for a slowly increasing population.

It so happens that the earliest human settlement site yet discovered in Scotland was found on the east coast of Rum, at the head of Loch Scresort, by Caroline Wickham-Jones during an archaeological dig sponsored by Historic Scotland in 1984-86. These excavations unearthed the remains of a Mesolithic (Middle Stone Age) settlement, dating from almost 9,000 years ago, just outside the contemporary village of Kinloch. It doesn't prove that Rum was in any way 'the cradle of mankind' in Scotland, but it's a nice 'first' for Rum to be able to boast while it lasts!

Mesolithic settlement: artist's impression

It was a happy accident of archaeology, which came about when a potato field just to the north of Kinloch Castle was being ploughed slightly more deeply than it had been before. The ploughman spotted large quantities of flaked stone and a beautiful barbed and tanged stone arrowhead, and immediately reported his find to staff of the Royal Commission on the Ancient and Historical Monuments of Scotland who were engaged in a survey of the island, and Caroline Wickham-Jones was called in.

The settlement turned out to be an extensive one: arcs of stake-holes indicated the locations of several shelters, and there were many traces of fires and broken hearth stones as well as numerous pits and hollows.

These first settlers had built small shelters from local materials like wood, brushwood and skins; they made hearths on which they could prepare food and even smoke meat and fish to keep for the winter. The climate at that time was moist and relatively warm – perhaps 2°C warmer than today. Much of the island was covered by open heathlands with shrubs of juniper and bog myrtle, but there was also light, low-canopied woodland, and copses of birch and hazel flourished in the more sheltered areas. Remains of carbonised hazelnut shells show that nuts were an important part of the early inhabitants' diet. There were no preserved bones to fill out the details of their menus, but seabirds and seals would have been valuable sources of oils and fat. Clothing was made from the skins of wild animals caught locally. While the hunters were away, other groups may have gone to the beaches of the north to gather shellfish, small animals and plants.

The most significant find at Kinloch was the discovery of an assemblage of more than 140,000 stone tools and waste flint-like material. The Mesolithic dwellers on Rum had made a variety of tools from stone, including microlithic arrowheads, scrapers, awls, blades and flakes. They used flint which they collected as pebbles from the beaches; but they also had access to a good knapping stone known as bloodstone, which has similar properties to flint. The source of the Rum bloodstone was on the west coast of the island, 10 kilometres away: Bloodstone Hill (Creag nan Steàrnan).

Good quality stone for tools is rare in Scotland, and the bloodstone must have made Rum very special to the early inhabitants of the western seaboard. We know from archaeological sites elsewhere that people from many of the surrounding islands and the adjoining mainland used bloodstone from Rum for their tools.

The first settlers of Scotland did not live in one place all the year round. They were hunter-gatherers, and the Kinloch site fitted this nomadic life-style perfectly. It was never a permanent settlement; but it was an ideal location because it was easily accessible and could provide ample resources for a large seasonal encampment. For people with boats, like the Mesolithic settlers, Rum was at the very heart of human life off the west coast of Scotland – probably one of a number of seasonal settlements of hunter-gatherers in the Hebrides.

The Kinloch encampment provided a home base from which small parties of hunters could set out across Rum, while others took boats to neighbouring islands and fishing grounds, carrying supplies of bloodstone implements to barter with their neighbours.

The Kinloch settlement site was used on and off for at least a thousand years during the Mesolithic period, but it seems to have been abandoned some 7,500 years ago. Nevertheless, it is unlikely that Rum was ever completely deserted by its prehistoric population. Traces of early settlement are extremely fragile, and they are always difficult to find; but despite the meagre information available there are hints that there were people on Rum. There is a broad but shallow cave at Bàgh na h-Uamha, on the east coast of the island, whose floor is covered by a deep midden deposit containing seashells and the bones of sheep, deer, horses, seals and seabirds which may go back to the Mesolithic period; the artefacts from the surface of the midden, however, are of much later date, and may indicate the presence of Norse visitors or settlers (see CHAPTER 3).

Neolithic and after

During the archaeological excavations at Kinloch, traces were discovered of the activities of the early Neolithic (New Stone Age) farmers who lived and worked on Rum from about 3,000 BC. This evidence included the so-called 'Rum brew': pollen remains from inside a potsherd suggested that these early farmers brewed a potion made from oats and barley flavoured with heather honey, meadowsweet and bog myrtle – either to drink, or to keep the midges at bay!

No settlement from this date has yet been found, but some evidence of later prehistoric inhabitants has come to light. Stray arrowheads and other stone tools have been picked up at various points on the island. In 1963 a schoolboy found a bloodstone arrowhead on the beach at Samhnan Insir, near Kilmory. In August 1982 a young geologist who was engaged in mapping the complex igneous rocks of Hallival picked up an arrowhead of white siliceous stone.

Although few vestiges remain of the presence of the early settlers of Rum they were certainly there. Red deer must have been a draw as a source of food, even after the early farmers brought in their own cattle and sheep and started clearing the land down to the sea for their crops.

Other monuments on the island indicate permanent settlement, such as the mounds at Guirdil, Kilmory, Harris and A' Bhrìdeanach which have been interpreted as Bronze Age cairns (c.1,000 BC); these suggest that there were local settled communities which needed a place to bury their dead. Traces of circular huts have also been identified by archaeologists at several places on Rum, such as Harris, and these too may date back to the Bronze Age. Several of these prehistoric structures have now been scheduled by Historic Scotland, and others are coming to light as survey efforts are intensified.

In common with the rest of Scotland, life on Rum began to change with the start of the Iron Age (400 BC onwards in the Hebrides). The promontory forts at Kilmory and Shellesder (between 2,500 and 1,500 years old) were built in obviously defensive locations, which suggest that a new degree of uncertainty had come into community life on the island, with new social hierarchies and power structures, by the start of the Christian era.

The history of human settlement on Rum is of considerable significance. The island was surveyed and catalogued in 1983 by the Royal Commission on the Ancient and Historical Monuments of Scotland, which found an impressive legacy of almost 200 archaeological sites and monuments. Further fieldwork in 1995 by Historic Scotland culminated in a report which described the archaeology of Rum as 'remarkable' and highlighted 17 sites, which have now been scheduled under the Ancient Monuments and Archaeological Areas Act 1979 as being of national importance.

CHAPTER 3

Lords of the Isle

THE MANY ARCHAEOLOGICAL sites and monuments are given context and colour by the documentary evidence as the story of Rum moves into the Christian era.

Early Christianity

In the sixth and seventh centuries AD, monks of the early Christian church founded by St Patrick in Ireland would launch themselves in their hide-covered *currachs* to spread the gospel. Others would set sail into unknown waters in search of some empty island on which they could live out the rest of their lives in humility and penitence as hermits. It was during this heroic age of Irish Christianity that St Columba (521-97) founded a monastery on Iona which became a great centre of Celtic Christianity; and from Iona others followed his example and carried the word in all directions.

There seems to have been some sort of hermitage on Rum as early as the seventh century, closely associated with Columban Christianity on Iona. Irish sources refer to an intellectual ascetic, St Beccán 'of Rum', who was known for his poems about Columba in the 630s and whose death was recorded in 677 AD. He may have spent some time on the island as a hermit whose cell was possibly situated in the south-west corner of the island in the area which the Vikings were to name Papadil – 'priests' dale'.

The Bàgh na h-Uamha cross

There is other, more tangible evidence of an early Christian presence on the island in the shape of two stones incised with crosses and seemingly dating from the 7th or 8th centuries. One water-worn sandstone pillar was found partly buried in the shingle beach at Bàgh na h-Uamha in 1977 and was re-erected above high-water mark in 1982. High up on one face is an incised equal-armed cross, set on a tall pedestal. This simple motif is found in other Celtic carvings and manuscripts, but it occurs first on pilgrim souvenirs from the Holy Land, representing the Cross set up by the Emperor Constantine on the site of Golgotha.

The other stone was found lying in the small burial-ground at Kilmory in 1885. It is a sandstone pillar on which is carved what is known as a 'marigold cross'; this much more elaborate motif consists of a cross-of-arcs within a peripheral bead-moulding on a pedestal, and the 'petals' dividing the cross-arms form a saltire. On the back of the slab there is a much plainer sunken Latin cross. This stone is still to be found in the burial-ground, lying face down.

Kilmory, in the north of the island, was an important area of early settlement, and the pillar would perhaps have had a public function as a focus for preaching and worship as well as burial, whereas the stone at Bàgh na h-Uamha is likely to have had a more private role. The name 'Kilmory' ('Church of Maelrubha') indicates that there was once a chapel in the vicinity dedicated to the Irish St Maelrubha of Applecross: indeed, a chapel on Rum was mentioned, but not identified, by Martin Martin (*A Description of the Western Isles of Scotland*) in 1703.

Norse rule

From early in the Viking Age (800-1100 AD) the Scottish islands came under Scandinavian rule: a Norse fiefdom which extended down the west coast from Shetland and Orkney (*North Islands*), through the Hebrides (*South Islands)* to the Isle of Man. Rum was clearly known to the Norsemen, but probably as sailors rather than settlers. There is no mention of it in the extensive medieval literature of the Norsemen, so we do not know if they had a name of their own for it, but many of the present place-names – particularly of the main hills (-val) and glens (-dal) – betray their Norse derivations: Ainshval (Rocky-ridge Hill), Askival (Spear Hill), Barkeval (Precipice Hill), Dibidil (Deep Dale), Hallival (Ledge Hill), Papadil (Priests' Dale), Ruinsival (Rock-pile Hill), Trollaval (Trolls' Hill). Many of these landscape features are conspicuous from the sea, and so provided useful landmarks for navigators plying the Hebridean seas.

It is impossible to say whether the Norsemen colonised Rum. The only archaeological evidence which has come to light consists of a double burial cist, assumed to be of Scandinavian origin, which was found at Bàgh na h-Uamha in 1949, and a small circular gaming piece of narwhal ivory, decorated with a delicate interlace pattern, which was found in the cave nearby (it is now in the Royal Museum in Edinburgh). But there are many place-names which combine Norse and Gaelic elements, which suggest that itinerant Norsemen might have settled and integrated with the indigenous people.

The 'marigold' cross in the burial-ground at Kilmory

Whether colonised or not, Rum remained, with the rest of the Hebrides, under Norse dominion until 1156, when Somerled of Argyll, a chieftain of mixed Norse and Celtic blood (his name derived from the Norse *Sumarlidi*, meaning 'Summer Warrior'), assumed authority over the southern islands. His descendants, the MacRuaris, were a powerful, if rebellious, naval force in Scotland. When King Alexander II sacked the islands in 1249 in an attempt to wrest the Hebrides from Norwegian control, the affronted MacRuaris sought Norse aid. King Håkon the Old of Norway brought a large fleet in 1263 in an attempt to restore Norwegian authority, but the expedition returned to Norway after an inconclusive skirmish on the beach at Largs in October 1263. Håkon the Old died in Orkney on the way home, and the Hebrides were formally ceded to the Scottish crown in 1266 under the Treaty of Perth.

When Robert the Bruce was fighting for the Scottish throne one of his most prominent Hebridean supporters was Angus Og, a direct descendant of Somerled. For his loyal service at the Battle of Bannockburn in 1314 he was granted vast lands in the west Highlands and Islands, stretching from the Butt of Lewis to Islay in addition to extensive mainland territories. His son and successor, 'Good' John of Islay, declared himself 'Lord of the Isles', and augmented his lands through marriage to his third cousin, Amy, heiress of the MacRuaris. Their son, Ranald, was the progenitor of the Clanranald chieftaincy, and inherited the bulk of the former MacRuari lands, including the islands of Rum and Eigg.

The Macleans of Coll

The Macleans of Duart, on Mull, were one of the clans who enjoyed the patronage of the Lordship of the Isles. In 1499 John Garbh, son of the seventh chief of the Macleans of Duart, demanded an inheritance from Alexander, the 3rd Lord of the Isles, who grudgingly gave him the island of Coll – an arrangement which was granted royal assent by King James II. Local tradition maintains that John Garbh Maclean later acquired the island of Rum from Clanranald in exchange for a fine-looking galley; Clanranald regretted the deal when the vessel's timbers proved to be rotten, and refused to confirm the sale, but the high-handed Maclean enforced the 'bargain' by holding Clanranald prisoner on Coll for nine months until the disputed succession to the island was conceded.

The powerful and unruly Lords of the Isles remained a constant threat to the Scottish throne until James IV managed to gain the upper hand, and declared their lands forfeit to the Crown in 1493. Only when the clans had submitted to the crown were their estates restored; this made the Macleans of Coll consider themselves independent of the Duart family, and they attempted to sever all ties of fealty. Maclean of Duart was so outraged that he launched devastating retribution on the Coll lands: in 1588, with the support of 100 Spanish marines from the Spanish Armada galleon *Florencia* which had sought shelter in Tobermory bay before sinking, he ravaged Rum and the other Small Isles 'in maist barbarous, shameful and cruell manner... not sparing the pupills and infants'.

When King James VI eventually subdued the wild Hebrides he commissioned a detailed *Description* of them (c.1580). This noted that there were only two townships on Rum, which could raise no more than six or seven fighting men (compared with 60 from Eigg). Rum was, said the Report, 'an ile of small profit... the hills and waist glennis are commodious only for the hunting of deir'. By the end of the 18th century, however, the deer population on Rum was extinct (see CHAPTERS 4 & 11).

The people

The earliest documentary record about Rum is found in John of Fordun's 14th century *Chronica gentis Scottorum*, which says that there were 'few inhabitants' on the island at that time. King James VI's report on Rum around 1580, with its reference to only six or seven fighting men, indicates that the population at the end of the 16th century cannot have been much larger; certainly, it must have suffered grievously during the punitive clan raids by Maclean of Duart. Franciscan missionaries visiting Rum in 1625 considered it 'so wild and mountainous as to make habitation difficult'.

Between 1585 and 1596 Timothy Pont travelled over a surprisingly large amount of the wildest and least accessible parts of Scotland, making a series of sketches intended as a basis for the first ever cartographical survey of Scotland; these sketches weren't published in a scholarly edition until 1989, but they were used in a simplified (and sometimes distorted) form by the Dutch cartographer Jan Blaeu as part of his atlas of the known world published in Amsterdam in 1654, *Theatrum Orbis Terrarum, sive Atlas Novus*. This 'New Atlas' located townships at Kilmory and Harris. In 1703, Martin Martin noted the existence of a chapel on Rum.

Until 1700, therefore, Rum seems to have been sparsely populated. The 18th century, however, saw a huge increase in the population of Rum. In 1728 the Society for the Propagation of Christian Knowledge recorded 152 persons over the age of five on Rum – a total population, perhaps, of 180. John Walker, in his *Report on the Hebrides of 1764 and 1771*, found that Rum had 304 inhabitants, in 57 families. This figure had soared, according to the 1796 *Old Statistical Account of Scotland*, to a peak of 443 in 1795.

The steep population rise in the 18th century was the product of several factors. For one thing, clan warfare had come to an end after the suppression of the Jacobite Risings of 1715 and 1745, bringing relative peace and security to the islanders. For another, inoculation against smallpox had become widely available in Scotland. There is no evidence that the people on Rum were inoculated at this time; but John Walker noted in 1764 how devastating a smallpox epidemic could be on an island like Rum:

> The Island was then accounted populous, as it had not been visited by the Small Pox for 29 years; for by this Disease upon former Occasions, it had been almost depopulate.

John Walker recorded his surprise at the size of the population:

> Such a Number of People, living in the way of Husbandry, upon so small a property is not perhaps to be found anywhere else in Europe.

It seems that cultivation itself may have been new as a widespread occupation on Rum in the 18th century. Walker recorded an old man on the island who had just died at the age of 103, and who had lived to 50 before he had ever tasted bread; until then he had lived on fish, milk and other animal produce:

> I was even told, that this old man used frequently to remind the younger People, of the simple and hardy Fare of former Times, used to upbraid them with their Indulgence in the Article of Bread, and judged it unmanly in them to toil like Slaves with their Spades, for the production of such an unnecessary Piece of Luxury.

In addition, a new 'convenience' food had been introduced to the Highlands in the middle of the 18th century – the potato.

The population boom on Rum mirrored the rapid growth of the rural population in the Highlands and Islands overall, and must have been well above the sustainable carrying capacity of the island. Indeed, after the peak figure of 443 the population began to decline in the early 19th century, by voluntary emigration and by enlistment in the armies fighting Napoleon.

How they lived then

A young Cambridge geologist, Edward Daniel Clarke, has left a delightful pen-picture of what life was like on Rum in those days (*Life and remains of Edward Daniel Clarke DD*, 1834). In 1797 he landed at the small, remote settlement at Guirdil, a fertile, steep-sided glen dominated by the towering ramparts of Bloodstone Hill. An old man, bonnet in hand, invited Clarke's party to his cottage where they found 'a clean but homely cloth spread upon a board between two beds, which served us for chairs, upon which was placed a collation of cream, eggs, new milk, cheese, oat-cakes and several bottles of fine, old Lisbon wine' (the last had been salvaged from a wrecked ship).

Nearly twenty years later the geologist John MacCulloch was storm-bound at Guirdil where he, too, was 'devoured by kindness' (*The Highlands and Western Islands of Scotland*, 1824). He and his crew fell in with the nearest Maclean who could converse in English and were provided with such fare as the house afforded:

> The neighbours had come to see the strangers... There was an old fiddle hanging up in a corner, very crazy in the pegs and in the intestines, but still practicable... A ball here requires no great preparations... The lassies had no shoes and marvellous little petticoat; but to compensate for these deficiencies they had an abundance of activity and good will... Where shall I go into such a house in England, find such manners and such conversation... and see such smoky shelves covered not only with the books of the ancients, but of the moderns... well thumbed and well talked of?

The ceilidh became prolonged 'in tender pity to the prettiest girl of the party, who had been sudden and quick in falling in love with a handsome lad belonging to my crew, and was weeping bitterly at the thoughts of parting.'

John MacCulloch's overall view of Rum as a whole was distinctly unromantic, however:

> There is a great deal of stormy magnificence about the lofty cliffs, as there is generally all round the shores of Rum; and they are, in most places, as abrupt as they are inaccessible from the sea. The interior is one heap of rude mountains, scarcely possessing an acre of level land. It is the wildest and most repulsive of all the islands. The outlines of Hallival and Haskeval are indeed elegant and render the island a beautiful and striking object from the sea....
>
> If it is not always bad weather in Rum, it cannot be good very often.

On this 'wildest and most repulsive of all the islands', everyday life was anything but easy. In 1771 the English naturalist Thomas Pennant had visited Rum and found that the island maintained 59 families grouped in nine small clachans (settlements) around the coast (*A tour in Scotland and voyage to the Hebrides*, 1772). These are named on Langland's map of Argyll (1801) as 'Kilmorry, Sandanisker, Camas Pleiseag, Kinlochscresort, Cove (Bàgh na h-Uamha), Glendibble, Pappadill, Harris and Guidle'. Pennant described the houses he found at Kinloch:

> [There were] a dozen houses, thick-walled and with low roofs of thatch... [Most possessed] neither windows or chimneys; a little hole on one side gave an exit to the smoke: the fire is made on the floor beneath; above hangs a rope, with the pot-hook at the end to hold the vessel that contains their hard fare, a little fish, milk or potatoes.

Harris was the largest single settlement, comprising about 30 of these 'blackhouses' clustered together behind the raised beach from which they derived shelter from the prevailing winds. Kilmory had about 20 houses, and included the only known communal graveyard on Rum. The soils at Harris and Kilmory are relatively deeper and richer, and the climate somewhat drier, than on the eastern side of the island. Kinloch did not become a primary settlement until the 19th century. The

An old blackhouse on Rum

ruins of something like 100 blackhouses are still discernible on Rum.

The extensive remains of the abandoned pre-Clearance settlement on the slopes facing Harris bay present a striking and evocative impression of a bygone age, and have been scheduled by Historic Scotland as a vivid document of domestic and social life on Rum prior to the Clearances. Around the mouth of the Glen Duian river are laid out the ruins of at least 37 buildings and enclosures, including blackhouses and barns, and their associated fields.

The islanders relied on a form of subsistence farming which allowed life to be sustained through simple cultivation and stock management. The prevailing system of agriculture was the so-called 'runrig', which enabled the land to be allocated annually so as to offer everyone a fair chance at the best of it. Each household held a share in the communal grazings, and helped one another in many seasonal tasks, to ensure that the oldest inhabitants weren't disadvantaged.

The method of tillage was in raised cultivation strips (*feannagan*) known as 'lazybeds' – a real misnomer, this, because the work was backbreaking. Parallel ditches were dug with foot-spades and the meagre soil was heaped up into ridges, leaving the drainage ditches in between, doubling the thickness of the soil. These 'lazybed' ridges, fertilised with seaweed or soot-impregnated thatch, provided a soil depth sufficient for oats, bere barley or (latterly) potatoes to be grown. Low drystane walls kept the livestock away from the precious crops. Some garden produce was grown in small enclosed kailyards, as was winter fodder.

In the summer months the women and children would herd the sheep and cattle to summer pasturage in the hills ('transhumance'); there

Pre-Clearances runrig (lazybed) fields at Harris

they lived in small turf and stone huts called 'shielings', built on the slopes of the hills, nestling singly or in groups close to a burn with good grazing nearby. The remains of more than 400 shielings, some of them in an excellent state of preservation, are to be found all over the island.

The islanders kept black cattle (ancestors of the contemporary black Highland cattle) and small native sheep, not unlike the St Kilda sheep of today. These were milked at the shielings so that butter and cheese could be laid in for the winter. Thomas Pennant noted in 1772 that 'the mutton here is small but the most delicate in our dominions... the natives kill a few [sheep], and also of cows to salt for winter provisions'. The *Old Statistical Account of Scotland* in 1796 said that 'in Rum, there is a considerable number of small native sheep; their flesh is delicious, and their wool is valuable'.

Another welcome addition to the diet was the summer supply of fat young Manx shearwaters (*fachachs*), harvested from nesting burrows in Rum's mountain-top colonies: 'the most delicate birds to be eaten... except that they doe taste oyld.' (Timothy Pont, in 1596). (See CHAPTER 10)

Some goats were kept, too; their descendants still range wild along the remote sea-cliffs of the islands. They also owned ponies as beasts of burden. Rum ponies were noted by Pennant in 1772; according to Dr Johnson in 1775 they were 'very small, but a breed eminent for beauty' (see CHAPTER 12).

The surrounding seas were full of fish, mainly herring, cod and ling, but the coastline and the ever-moving sea made landing too difficult for fishing to be developed as an industry, and 'the inhabitants being ill provided in fishing materials, seldom catch a competency for their own families' (*Old Statistical Account of Scotland*). Some fish were landed at Kinloch, however, which was the only sheltered harbour. Hugh Miller, the pioneer Scottish geologist and stonemason who cruised the Hebrides in the yacht *Betsey* in 1844-45 (*The Cruise of the Betsey*, 1879), noted the remains of an old stone-and-turf structure which created an artificial pool in which to trap fish on receding tides. [This was situated in front of the modern school.]

But despite the apparent bounty of Nature, survival on Rum was a harsh and chancy business. Thomas Pennant in 1772 had no illusions about it:

> The produce of the crops very rarely are in any proportion to the wants of the inhabitants... The people are a well-made and well-looking race but carry famine in their aspect. [They] are often a whole summer without a grain in the island which they regret not on their own account but for the sake of their poor babes. In the present economy there is no prospect of any improvement.

The Rum Clearances

With so many inhabitants the island's resources were severely strained. The owner of Rum, the clan chief, **Alexander Maclean**, 14th of Coll, was renowned as 'a man of independent character, and greatly beloved for his benevolent and generous disposition', but there were limits to his benevolence. The Napoleonic wars had caused cattle prices to slump; the islanders were in arrears with their rents, and resented his attempts to improve their sheep husbandry; furthermore, his own finances had been dealt a blow by a disastrous investment: in 1814 he had paid £9,975 for the island of Muck, hoping to make money out of its plentiful supplies of kelp (a type of seaweed): kelp was used to make soda ash for explosives, and with the Napoleonic War in full swing there was a ready market for the product. With the end of the war in 1815, however, demand fell abruptly and the trade collapsed.

Eventually Maclean (or more probably his hard-headed son, Hugh) resolved on a drastic remedy to recoup his losses: Rum was leased as a sheep-walk to a single tenant, **Dr Lachlan Maclean** of Gallanach on Coll, who was a kinsman by marriage. All the existing arable and grazing land would be required for maximum stocking. Dr Maclean got quotations for shipping 300 Rum folk to Nova Scotia. The lowest quotation (after some haggling) was £5.15s (£5.75) a head, and at Whitsun 1825 the islanders received a year's notice to quit. They were to be replaced by 8,000 Blackface sheep.

On 11 July 1826, 300 men, women and children were herded on board two ships, the *Dove of Harmony* and the *Highland Lad*, to be transported to Port Hawkesbury in Nova Scotia. The Clearance was supervised for Maclean of Coll by an Edinburgh lawyer, Alexander Hunter, who later admitted to a Government Select Committee on Emigration in 1827 that although some of the islanders accepted their fate, 'others were not very willing to leave the land of their ancestors.' John McMaister, a shepherd on Rum at the time, was less diplomatic: 50 years later he told of a scene 'of such stressful description that he would never be able to forget it till his dying day':

> The wild outcries of the men and the heart-breaking wails of the women and their children filled all the air between the mountainous shores of the bay.

The islanders' 37-day passage to the New World in confined, crowded and dirty quarters cannot have been a comfortable one. Maclean of Coll had provided each adult with 35 pints of water, 11 pounds of oatmeal, 3 1/2 pounds of bread or biscuit, half a pound of molasses, half a pound of pease or barley, and a quarter pound of butter. A few islanders were able to eke out these rations with some salt mutton and potatoes of their own.

Only 50 people now remained behind on Rum. But two years later, on 12 July 1828, they too were shipped off to the New World on the *St Lawrence*, along with 150 Maclean tenants from Muck. That left only one family of native islanders – eleventh-generation Macleans who proudly claimed direct descent from the Macleans of Coll themselves; this family lived in a blackhouse at Càrn nan Dòbhran (*The Otters' Cairn*) which is still in a good state of preservation on the southern shore of Loch Scresort in what is now the South Side Wood.

The wholesale clearance meant that Dr Maclean, the grazing tenant, now found himself deficient in shepherds to look after his 8,000 sheep. He managed to divert a dozen families who were being 'cleared' from Mull and from Bracadale on Skye and had them shipped to Rum, where five of the families built thatched cottages in the township of Port nan Carannan (*Port of the Turnings*) on 'a bit of morass' on the southern shore of Loch Scresort, looking across the sea to Skye. By 1831 Rum supported a community of 134 souls; but by 1861 the families from Skye had moved into a cluster of cottages at Kinloch – 'The Town', as it came to be called – and Port nan Carannan was abandoned.

Meanwhile Dr Maclean 'spared no expense in his improvements, which exhibited both taste and judgement', according to the *New Statistical Account of Scotland*. He erected a lodge at Kinloch – Kinloch House, called *Tigh Mor* ('the Big House') by the islanders – which was later described by the Lancashire poet Edwin Waugh in his book *The Limping Pilgrim, on his Wanderings* (1883):

> It is a plain, strongly-built stone house, with a steep roof, and with a porch, and with a small wing at each end, one of which is used as a gun room and the other as a kitchen. The rear and ends of the house

are shaded by trees, and the lawn in front slopes gently down to the shore of the bay. The south side of the lawn is flanked by the garden, and the north side partly by trees and partly by a low-built, comfortable, whitewashed cottage, which is the second best upon the island and is the residence of the sheep farmer of the island.

The cottage, extensively renovated, is the oldest building on the island and is now the General Store/Post Office. Only the gateposts survive beneath the tall sycamores to indicate where Kinloch Lodge itself once stood.

The sycamores are part of a one-acre cluster of trees which Dr Maclean had planted at the back and sides of Kinloch House, and which Edwin Waugh later said was known to the islanders as 'The Park':

> Their fine, healthy appearance, now, is strong evidence of what might be done in these bare, mountainous Hebridean islands by plantation. This compact clump of wood at Kinloch House looks very striking, seen from the bay; and it looks all the more so because the rest of the island is as bare of trees as a lapstone... There is not another tree, worthy of the name, on all the island.

Not long after the Rum Clearances the price of mutton plummeted, and the sheep enterprise collapsed. Throughout the Highlands and Islands severe famine ensued; a public appeal in 1836 raised £50,000 'for the alleviation of distress amongst the inhabitants'. In an account of the problems, compiled by two members of the Statistical Society of Glasgow (*Remarks on the Evils at present Affecting the Highlands and Islands of Scotland*, 1838), there is a brief but bleak reference to Rum:

> Rum, which is one of the most rugged, bleak and barren of the Hebrides, is so peculiarly liable to violent storms of wind and rain, as, with the exception of a few hundred acres of low lying land, to afford no encouragement to the raising of crops on any part of its surface...
> It is occupied as a sheep farm by Dr Maclean, who, with his family and shepherds, and a few cotiers, forms its only inhabitants.

In 1839 Dr Maclean left Rum, bankrupt and penniless, and spent some time in Australia before retreating, an alcoholic, to a medical practice in Tobermory.

Six years later, in 1845, Maclean of Coll's son, Hugh, the 16th and last Maclean of Coll, put the island on the market. The geologist Hugh Miller visited it that year, and after a walk over the hills to Guirdil he noted:

> All was solitary. We could see among the deserted fields the grass-grown foundations of cottages razed to the ground; but the valley... had not even its single inhabited dwelling... it seemed as if man had done with it forever.... It did not seem as if the depopulation of Rum had tended much to anyone's advantage. A report went current at the time that the island was on the eve of being purchased by some wealthy Englishman, who purported converting it to a deer forest.

CHAPTER 4

A Sporting Estate

The Salisbury years

THE 'WEALTHY ENGLISHMAN' rumoured to be on the verge of purchasing Rum was the **2nd Marquis of Salisbury** (the father of the Victorian Prime Minister, the 3rd Marquis). The rumour proved to be correct: he bought the island for £26,455 in 1845. Salisbury embarked on
an extensive programme of 'improvements' to transform the island into
a typical Victorian Highland estate with an emphasis on
field sports. He kept about 5,000 of the sheep in nine
hirsels (areas of pasturage) at various locations
around the island; each hirsel was looked after
by a shepherd, and new cottages were built for
the shepherds. He built a new stone pier at Kinloch (which, unfortunately, dries out at low tide);
a track was made to Kilmory and to Harris where
there had only been paths before. Large tracts of
land were drained in an attempt at reclamation.
A circular lime-kiln was built at the head of
Loch Scresort, but this was soon abandoned and
is now a listed structure. A quarry was opened up
on Bloodstone Hill, where the earliest humans on
Rum had fashioned their arrowheads; Queen Victoria was later presented with a coffee table top
made of polished bloodstone from Rum.

A herd of red deer

But Salisbury's main interest was in the sporting potential of the
island, and he took several positive steps to improve its value – especially as a deer-stalking estate. The deer population on Rum had become
extinct by the end of the 18th century; Salisbury re-stocked the island,
initially with fallow deer but, increasingly, with red deer from Scottish
estates and English deer parks, and soon the red deer on Rum numbered
about 600. Other game was introduced, including mountain hares, par-
tridge and pheasant, but none survived for long. He tried to improve the
management of heathland for the benefit of red grouse; and like all Victorian estate-owners he ensured that birds of prey which might interfere
with his shooting were killed.

Salisbury also tried to improve the river systems for game fishing.
The most spectacular project was an ambitious scheme to transform the

Kinloch River into a first-class salmon and sea-trout river. It involved diverting the headwaters of the upper Kilmory (which flows north to Kilmory Bay) through a 300-metre rock-cut lade into the Kinloch River (which flows east into Loch Scresort) by means of a dam which would create a 'New Loch'. A force of 300 workmen from the surrounding islands laboured on the construction of a massive, curving stone-built dam; it was 10.5m thick at the base and nearly 6m in height, and about 60m in length. It took two years to construct, but the dam had been badly designed, presenting a concave surface to the dammed water instead of a convex one – and two days after the completion of the breastwork the dam burst under the pressure of the water. A huge flood surged down Kilmory Glen, scouring the floor of the glen and carrying tons of priceless topsoil to the sea, while £11,000 went down the drain. 'Salisbury's Dam' is now a scheduled historic monument.

In 1850 Salisbury conveyed the island to his eldest son, Viscount Cranborne, who in 1852 'gave assistance to' 55 islanders on Rum to emigrate to Canada. Among them were many of the Maclean family who had survived the previous Clearances. One son, Kenneth, continued to live near Kinloch, in the blackhouse at Càrn nan Dòbhran (*Otters' Cairn*) which had been the family home for 11 generations. He was 'a man of mark… who knew more about the unwritten traditions of Rum than any man living'. He identified for the Ordnance Survey in 1877 the only place-names surviving to this day.

By the 1850s the last two Skye families from Port nan Carannan had moved into the straggling cluster of cottages which made up 'The Town' at Kinloch, increasing the community there to some 40 souls; a handful of shepherd families lived in lonely cottages at Dibidil, Papadil, Guirdil, Harris and Kilmory. Viscount Cranborne maintained a steamship to transport sheep carcasses to Liverpool until about 1863, when he let the grazings (some 10,000 sheep) to a **Captain Campbell** of Ballinaby, on Islay.

The Campbell years

In 1866 Viscount Cranborne died and Rum passed to his younger brother, the future Conservative prime minister (the 3rd Marquis of Salisbury). In 1870 the island was sold to Farquhar Campbell of Aros, and it was probably this owner who built a shooting lodge at Kinloch 'for the accommodation of visitors during the shooting season' (Edwin Waugh, p 74):

> It is a plain, substantial house, of two storeys; and it is four rooms in length upon the ground floor… It is whitewashed outside; and it is known amongst the people of Rum by the name of 'Tigh Ban', or 'The White House'.

The White House is now the Scottish Natural Heritage office on

The White House, Kinloch, c. 1910

Rum and the residence of the Reserve Manager.

During much of the Campbell ownership, tenant farmers from Skye occupied Kinloch Lodge and employed many islanders as farm labourers and shepherds. From 1879 the shooting on the island was being let, at £800 per annum, to a Mr John Bullough, a wealthy industrialist from Lancashire who was the great friend and patron of Edwin Waugh (see CHAPTER 5).

The population of the island had risen again to nearly 90 by this time. Several of the families in the remoter areas found lodgings for their children in Kinloch where they could attend the school during the week. One fourteen-year-old boy, Kenneth Chisholm – 'as hard and shaggy as a Highland colt' – stayed with old Kenneth Maclean at Càrn nan Dòbhran; each Saturday he would walk whistling back to his home at Papadil nine miles away, 'as content as a king, carrying with him into that secluded spot all the news of the busy world upon the shore of Scresort Bay.'

The Kilmory shepherd, Murdo Matheson, was to quit the island under tragic circumstances. In April 1871 his seven-month-old son died. Two years later, within three September days, diphtheria claimed five more of his children. With their six surviving children Murdo and Christina Matheson emigrated to New Zealand where they found employment until their sons were able to set up on their own. The eldest, Dougal, spent the winter exploring South Island, where he found and named Lake Matheson, renowned for its picture-postcard reflection of

Rum for sale: advertisement in *The Times*, 1886

Mount Cook. Over the years, descendants of the family have returned to the tiny burial ground at Kilmory to pay their respects at the children's melancholy gravestone.

Farquhar Campbell died in 1882 and Rum passed to his cousin, James Hunter Campbell of Ormsary, who soon decided to sell it. It was put up for auction in London on June 18, 1886, as part of an IMPORTANT SALE OF SCOTCH ESTATES, and fulsomely described in an advertisement in *The Times* of 5 June:

... the magnificent sporting ISLAND OF RUM which, being the most picturesque of the islands which lie off the West Coast of Scotland, is altogether a property of exceptional attractions. The sporting capabilities are unsurpassed, and as a sporting estate it has at present few equals. Besides the sporting amenities it affords a very handsome rental...

The game consists of red and fallow deer, grouse, partridges, woodcock, snipe, and the great variety of wildfowl of the West Hebrides. The deer and sheep are both well known as being some of the heaviest in Scotland. The fishings are excellent, there being on the island numerous lochs fully stocked with trout, and streams affording capital seatrout fishing during the season...

The population, some 60 or 70 in all, is composed of shepherds and workmen and their families, employed by the sheep farmer or by the estate.

There are no crofts...

The scenery of the Island of Rum is magnificent, and so unique a property is seldom on the market.

The naturalist J A Harvie-Brown apparently toyed with the idea of purchasing it; but one of his Edinburgh solicitor friends was scathing in his comments on it:

I cannot find in it one redeeming feature. Roads bad. Peats ditto. Lochs inaccessible. Rivers spoilt by artificial endeavour to improve on nature. No salmon. Difficulty of access, climate abominable and everything uncomfortable. Ugh! Ugh! I wouldn't live on the place tho' you gave me it for nothing.

CHAPTER 5

Enter the Bulloughs

IN MAY 1888, RUM WAS BOUGHT for £35,000[1] by an energetic Lancashire textile machinery industrialist called **John Bullough** (pronounced 'Buller'). Bullough already owned the 60,000-acre estate of Meggernie, in Glenlyon in Perthshire, but he wanted Rum as a private holiday resort; he had leased the lodge and sporting rights on the island from the Campbells since 1879 and had taken a great liking to the place.

From humble origins, and building on the inventive flair of his father, James Bullough (who started his working life as a handloom weaver), John Bullough had risen to become one of the wealthiest industrial magnates in the north of England.

The story of how the Victorian textile industry in Lancashire manufactured the money which was transmuted into an extravagant Edwardian castle on a remote island in the Hebrides is a fascinating one.

James Bullough (c. 1800-68)

The chronicle of the Bulloughs is also the chronicle of industrial Lancashire in the 19th century: a story of seething endeavour to make good, of a thirst for learning and of industrial turmoil as men and women fought to protect their jobs against the threat posed by new machinery.

James Bullough was the man who began the family ascent. He was one of the artisan inventors who drove the Lancashire textile industry to new heights. He was born at West Houghton, near Bolton, in about 1800 (there is some doubt about the precise date; his baptismal certificate is dated October 1803). The ornamental Bullough pedigree on display in Kinloch Castle rather dubiously attempts to trace the family roots

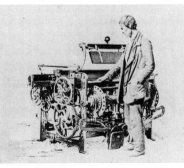

James Bullough (c.1800-68)

to a Stephen Bulhalgh who settled in Lancashire early in the 13th century and received grants of land; but there was no inherited wealth for the 19th century Bulloughs of West Houghton – far from it.

James was put to work as a handloom weaver at the age of seven,

---

[1]*The price paid by John Bullough has frequently been quoted as £150,000. The figure of £35,000 is confirmed by the deed of 'Disposition by James Hunter Campbell in favour of John Bullough', dated May 14, 1888.*

HOWARD & BULLOUGH, LIMITED.

GLOBE WORKS, ACCRINGTON.

The Globe Works, Accrington

long before the powerloom was in general use, when steam power was in its infancy and the processes of both spinning and weaving were still very primitive. It was also a time of feverish innovation and invention (hundreds of patents were to be taken out for the powerloom alone in the mid-Victorian years), when every 'improvement' provoked fear and anger among the workforce. Undeterred by the industrial crusades against the introduction of power-driven machines (he had witnessed an attack on a cotton factory in West Houghton), James Bullough quietly applied himself to improving the machinery on which he laboured. He invented and fitted to his own loom a simple but ingenious contrivance (the 'self-acting temple') which would inform him whenever the weft was broken: it consisted of a twisted lock of his sister's hair, formed into a loop, which would touch off a lever if the weft broke and set a warning bell in motion (the hair was later replaced with a delicate spring made by a Bolton watchmaker).

By the time powerlooms had become widespread, in the face of serious outbreaks of rioting and machinery-breaking, James Bullough had risen in his trade to the level of 'overlooker' at factories in Bolton, Bury and Preston. He had married a girl called Martha Smith in 1824, and had three sons and four daughters. He was still inventing improvements, not all of which proved effective. But in 1841, in partnership with another artisan inventor, William Kenworthy, he patented two inventions which were to revolutionise the weaving trade: an improved 'weft fork' stop motion (to stop the powerloom when the thread broke) and the 'roller temple', an improved method of keeping woven cloth at its proper width. In the following year he patented a 'loose reed motion', which allowed the lathe to swing backwards if the shuttle became trapped in the warps. Collectively, these developments made the powerloom a much more efficient machine, and eventually enabled their inventors to establish their own mills.

When the innovations were introduced into the Brookhouse Mills in Blackburn they were met with furious resistance by the mill-workers which culminated in the so-called Plug-Drawing Riots, and Bullough was forced to flee Blackburn.

Four years later he struck out for himself in the cotton industry. With a cousin from West Houghton (Adam Bullough) he started a factory at Waterside, near Darwen, and when that partnership was dissolved five years later he moved to Baxenden, where he took over two other mills.

The big breakthrough for the Bullough family came in the 1850s, when James teamed up with an entrepreneur called John Howard. John Howard was nearly 20 years younger than James, and in 1853 had founded the Globe Works in Accrington with a financial partner, James Bleakey. Not long afterwards his partner withdrew, for reasons now unknown, and Howard was now looking for another partner. James Bullough was by now a well-known entrepreneur in his own right: in 1856 an agreement was reached whereby James would provide the necessary capital and the title of the firm would be changed to Howard & Bullough. James also stipulated that his youngest son, John, who was 18 years old at the time, would become a partner in the firm: James had recognised his youngest son's inventiveness and talent and, when asked about this apparent favouritism, he replied that he had made provision for his older sons, Jack and Will, but 'the Globe's for John'. John Bullough was introduced to the firm in 1862 and became the principal partner in 1866.

When James Bullough joined Globe Works it was engaged mainly in jobbing work, with 150 employees and a weekly wages bill of £153. The company now turned its attention to loom-making. One of the key inventions which gave the fledgling Globe Works an immediate advantage over its competitors was a device known as the 'Slasher'; it was a refinement of an earlier invention for starching ('sizing') the warp, and trebled the output of each loom. It met stout resistance, of course, but by the end of the 1850s it was in place and fully accepted, and the Globe Works was on song.

James Bullough was a quiet, unassuming man. He was never happier than when pottering about in the mechanics' shop in the Globe Works, planning and contriving further improvements in the mechanical processes connected with the manufacturing of textile fabrics. He lived in the end house on Hill Street, Baxenden (popularly known as Bullough Row because it had been built by him in 1857 for the workers of Shoe Mill). His life-style was modest, and he became a kenspeckle figure in his habitual attire of top hat and clogs (albeit elaborately embroidered 'dandy clogs').

James died in Baxenden in 1868; his partner, John Howard, had died two years earlier. By then the management of the Globe Works had devolved upon James' youngest son, John Bullough.

John Bullough (1838-91)

It was to John Bullough that the remarkable growth of the Globe Works in Accrington was due. He had been born at Brookhouse, Blackburn, in 1838, the third son in a family of seven, and had always been earmarked by his father to take over the company. Like his father, John Bullough had a considerable flair for mechanical invention; but there the likeness ended. Where James Bullough was shy and retiring, John Bullough was ebullient and extrovert. Where James shunned the limelight, John liked nothing better than making speeches. James Bullough had had little schooling; John Bullough was given every chance of a good education at a Quaker school (Queenswood College in Hampshire), and at Glasgow University, where he studied Arts and developed a taste for music and literature but did not graduate.

As a businessman he showed astuteness and managerial skill. Under his direction, the works expanded and prospered. When he took over as head of Howard & Bullough the company employed 500 hands with an annual wages bill of £8,000; by 1871 the wage bill had risen to £30,000, and by 1874 to £39,000. Extension followed extension as the emphasis was changed from weaving to spinning. In 1876, on a visit to the United States, Bullough spotted a new kind of ring spindle at the American Exhibition and promptly bought the patent from its inventor 'for a considerable sum of money'. The Rabbeth ring spindle revolutionised the cotton spinning process, and its mass production from 1878 onwards revolutionised the Globe Works; every department was enlarged and the works were completely transformed. Within a few years, millions of Rabbeth spindles were being exported all over the world, and soon the Globe Works was employing 2,000 people.

Many of the other innovations at the time were John Bullough's own; of the scores of patents taken out from the Globe Works, no

John Bullough (1838-91)

fewer than 26 were registered in Bullough's name, besides a dozen more in association with others.

John Bullough was now an extremely wealthy man. He lived in a handsome mansion, The Rhyddings in Oswaldtwistle, having moved from The Laund in Accrington. Like so many Victorian entrepreneurs he gave generously to good causes: he established the Globe Works Technical School for his workforce, and helped to found the Accrington Mechanics' Institute. A keen sportsman all his days, he made large contributions to the local football and swimming clubs. He lavished money on the local Conservative party (he paid for the building of the Conservative Club) and became its chairman. He was an ardent supporter of Lord Salisbury:

A man of profound learning, the highest refinement, the personification of courtesy and urbanity, a model landlord universally beloved by those around him.

Although he never sought a career in politics he was elected to the Carlton Club, and there was nothing he enjoyed better than making vigorously partisan speeches at the drop of a hat: indeed, so proud was he of his political speeches that, soon after his death, his widow was to issue them 'for private circulation' in three handsome tooled-leather volumes, each 400 gilt-edged pages long.

John Bullough married twice. His first marriage, in 1868, was to Bertha Schmidlin, of Thun, near Berne, the daughter of a Swiss cotton manufacturer; they had a son, George, who was born in February 1870, and a daughter, Bertha (b. 1873). The marriage ended in bitter acrimony, and in September 1884, when George was 14 years old, John Bullough married again. His second wife was a much younger woman, Alexandria Marion, the daughter of Kenneth Mackenzie, a banker in Stornoway on the Isle of Lewis. They had a son, John, known as Ian, who was born in February 1886, and a daughter, Gladys (b. 1888).

Just before his second marriage, in 1884, John Bullough bought the 60,000-acre estate and 16th century castle of Meggernie in Glenlyon, Perthshire. It had been described in *The Times* as not only an attractive investment but as an exclusive retreat where 'a man of taste might have *carte blanche* in his own private wilderness, where all the elements of the picturesque are weighed in the wildest profusion'. The approach to the castle was through a magnificent avenue of lime trees, more than two miles long. The castle itself had 27 bedrooms, extensive stables, dog kennels and gardens, with 20,000 acres of shooting: they yielded bags of the order of 1,000 brace of grouse as well as black game, ptarmigan, red deer, roe deer, hares and rabbits, and there was good salmon-fishing in the River Lyon and Loch Lyon. An estate like Meggernie was the ultimate status symbol for the successful Victorian businessman. Here John Bullough was able to indulge his growing passion for shooting.

His second major land purchase in Scotland was Rum. To John Bullough, it was an island paradise. He had rented the shooting there since 1879, having heard of it from his hero, the Marquis of Salisbury. To facilitate access to his new domain he bought a sailing yacht, the *Mystery*, a 43-ton, 55-ft cutter which had been built in Cowes in 1862. On Rum he could entertain his business and sporting friends in some style and comfort. Here he enjoyed the company of his protégé, the local poet Edwin Waugh, who was hailed at the time as Lancashire's answer to Robert Burns; Waugh spent several summers on Rum in the 1880s, and published a long and affectionate description of the island in his book

The Limping Pilgrim, on his Wanderings (1883).

With his purchase of Meggernie and Rum, and his second marriage, Bullough applied himself less diligently to his business affairs and began to live the life of a landed laird. His speeches and writings betray both a cloying sentimentality and an extraordinary insensitivity towards the history and culture of his Highland and island tenantry. In a letter to *The Times* (28 January, 1888), proudly reprinted among his speeches, he attacked 'the indolent, ignorant and poor crofter' and defended the incomer lowland farmers as 'men of energy, intelligence and capital':

> Meanwhile, the well-clad, well-fed, pampered crofter continues to loaf away his time while his wife does the work, reserving his small stock of energy for attacks on his neighbours' property and demonstrations against the officers of the law.

In an appendix to the third volume of the Speeches, his widow included reams of romantic doggerel he had written about Rum 'on the hillside near some bonnie highland burn and during the enjoyment of his after-luncheon cigar':

> And year by year, as round we come
> To greet our grand old Father Rum,
> He'll o'er and o'er renew his blessing
> Well pleased to see us to him pressing.

When Bullough bought Rum he retained only three of the island families (there are no records of the fate of the others), and brought in fresh staff from other islands and from his Meggernie estate. He kept the sheep-grazing, and built shepherds' cottages at Kilmory, Harris, Guirdil and Dibidil. He also built comfortable shooting lodges at Harris and at Papadil, and continued to import stags from English deer-parks to improve the stock of red deer; and in 1889, with the guidance of the naturalist J A Harvie-Brown, who knew the island well, he embarked on a large-scale tree-planting programme (80,000 trees) around Loch Scresort.

John Bullough did not have long in which to enjoy his private kingdom on Rum. In February 1891, at the age of 53, he died in the Hotel Metropole in London from congestion of the lungs; he had been on his way with his new family to Monte Carlo for some weeks of Mediterranean warmth, but was caught in a London pea-souper which brought about his fatal illness. He died leaving personal estate in the United Kingdom of £1,228,183 (consisting mainly of the value of his shares in Howard & Bullough), in addition to his properties in Scotland and Lancashire. After making reasonable provision for his widow[1] and his two daughters, the Meggernie estate was left in trust to his 5-year-old son, Ian, and the island of Rum was bequeathed to his elder son, George, who was then three days short of his 21st birthday. The Globe Works in Accrington was to be converted into a limited liability company and the whole of the share capital was to be divided equally between George and Ian – a substantial fortune valued at £500,000 each.[1]

With John Bullough's death, and George Bullough's huge inheritance, a bizarre new chapter opened in the story of Rum.

Sir George Bullough (1870-1939)

George Bullough was half-way through a round-the-world cruise when he was summoned home by the news of his father's unexpected and untimely death. He discovered that, while his 5-year-old half-brother Ian had inherited Meggernie, he himself had inherited not just the island of Rum and the yacht (the cutter, *Mystery*) but also half of the family business in Accrington (Howard & Bullough), and the family home in Lancashire (The Rhyddings in Oswaldtwistle).

The world cruise on which young George learned of his inheritance has been the subject of much speculation. Rumour has it that he had been developing a rather 'close relationship' with his young stepmother, Alexandria, whom his father had married in 1884, and that as a result he had been packed off by his father, out of harm's way. There is no way, now, of confirming or denying that story: the 'official' version is that his father and stepmother had given George a two-year round-the-world cruise with his friends to celebrate his forthcoming 21st birthday. What is also open to speculation is whether they travelled on the *Mystery* (which seems rather small for such an ambitious voyage), or whether a larger vessel was chartered.

It was during this overseas cruise – the first of several he would make – that George started amassing the collection of oriental *objets d'art* and World Tour souvenir bric-a-brac which would adorn the future Kinloch Castle.

Sir George Bullough (1870-1939)

As a young man George Bullough emerges as an attractive if somewhat raffish figure. He was the archetypal example of the scion of third-generation wealth establishing himself in top society. Educated at Harrow, where he made a reputation for his love of sport and horse-riding, he was at first employed at his father's Globe Works to learn the fami-

[1] *In 1892 Alexandria Bullough married Lt Colonel John Beechy, and they had further children.*

The tiled back wall of the original Bullough vault at Harris

ly business. Very tall (he was well over six feet), handsome and well-built, he was as enthusiastic a sportsman as his father had been, and now, a dashing young cavalry-officer backed by huge wealth, he launched himself into the social life of London and started spending his vast inheritance with a will. But he made no attempt to disguise the source of his money: in Kinloch Castle he was to display prominently two illuminated testimonials to his father, one (in 1872) from his work-force for reducing the working hours without loss of wages to 54 hours a week, the other (in 1876) from the cotton manufacturers of the district 'to recognise the great benefits which your improvements in Machinery for Manufacturing purposes have accomplished'. His coat of arms as a baronet displayed bulls' heads (for Bullough) and bees, to represent industry.

Meanwhile Howard & Bullough was converted into a private limited company, as his father's will had stipulated. In 1893 it expanded to the United States as the Howard & Bullough American Machine Co Ltd, and established works at Pawtucket, Rhode Island. In the following year Howard & Bullough became a public company with capital of £1,000,000 and George Bullough as chairman of directors.[1]

The first building operation which George undertook on Rum was to construct a fitting burial-place for his father – a mausoleum at Harris. In the event he built two. The first took the form of an arched cruciform vault cut into the hillside, lined with coloured monogrammed ceramics. Here he laid the coffin of his father. The story goes, however, that an acquaintance (said to have been a correspondent from *The Times* being shown around the island) likened the tiled mosaic interior to a public lavatory at Waterloo Station; George promptly built a much more substantial family mausoleum nearby in the style of an open Doric temple. It consists of a concrete plinth approached by broad shallow steps on each of four rectangular sides; eighteen round pillars support a massive slated roof. Here John Bullough's body was re-interred in a sandstone table-tomb. The original tomb in the hillside was blown up with dynamite; the rear wall is still visible with its facing of mosaic tiles in a convoluted floral pattern, and bearing the initials JB.

The Bullough Mausoleum at Harris

George registered the *Mystery* with the Royal Clyde Yacht Club in 1893. Two years later, in 1895, he made his first major inroad into his fortune with the purchase of a floating palace: it was a luxurious twin-decked schooner-rigged steam yacht, 670 tons gross and 221ft overall, called the *Maria*, which had been built two years previously at the Glasgow yard of Napier, Shanks and Bell for a customer in Torquay. George renamed it the *Rhouma*. It was a vessel built in the grand style, with space even for a twelve-piece orchestra. He also bought a two-ton wooden cutter, the *Morna*, presumably to operate as a tender for the *Rhouma* in Loch Scresort.

But even a magnificent ocean-striding yacht was not sufficient for George Bullough, and in 1897, at the age of 27, he laid the foundation stone for what was to become his most visible legacy to Rum – Kinloch Castle.

---

¹ *The company continued to prosper and expand, right up to the outbreak of the First World War, when it had a workforce of 5,000. After the war it began to suffer a long, slow decline, and in 1931 it formed the Textile Machinery Makers group, of which Sir George was president. In the Second World War the entire production at the Globe Works was given over to munitions and military equipment, and the workforce was increased to 6,000. But in the post-war years the company never recovered its industrial eminence. In 1970 it became Platt International (Platt Saco Lowell in 1975), and the renowned Howard & Bullough name disappeared. In 1982 Platt Saco Lowell went into receivership. The area which had once been a hive of industrial activity and the largest single employer in the town disintegrated into industrial dereliction. In the final act, the Globe Works was demolished (apart from the corner office block) in 1995/96; the vast site is now being redeveloped by Hyndburn District Council as an office, hotel and leisure complex.*

CHAPTER 6

Kinloch Castle

NEARLY ALL VISITORS TO RUM nowadays arrive by ferry into Loch Scresort, on the island's east coast. As you wait for the tide to approach the pier, or for the island tender boat to meet the ferry, the most obvious elements in the landscape are the thick woodlands around the shore with a scatter of whitewashed houses among them, and Kinloch Castle standing proud at the head of the bay.

Kinloch Castle: watercolour by Byron Cooper (1902)

This astonishing red sandstone edifice was completed in 1900. 'Bizarre, battlemented and pseudo-baronial' – that is how Kenneth Williamson described it in a chapter of his book on the Hebrides (*A Mosaic of Islands*, by Kenneth Williamson & J. Morton Boyd, 1963). Bizarre it certainly is, to find such an extraordinary building on an isolated Hebridean island; but the story behind the castle is no less piquant.

The making of the Castle

George Bullough had shot his first stag on Rum (a six-pointer weighing 12 stones) in Glen Harris on Boxing Day, 1888, at the age of 18, and loved the island as devotedly as his father had done. But George wanted a much more palatial residence for himself and his army and society friends than Kinloch House, which was now becoming very dilapidated. So he resolved to build himself a castle.

Although he would have preferred Harris to Kinloch as a location (the climate is drier on the west coast, and the land more fertile), he chose Kinloch because Scresort Bay offered the only safe anchorage for his yacht. The architects he selected were Leeming & Leeming, who had designed the extension to the Admiralty building in Horse Guards Parade and Leeds Market Hall. Their design was for a square, crenellated, two-storey mansion around a central courtyard with round towers at each corner, and a square platformed tower with a round turret off-centre over the east-facng entrance. It is said that he wanted a castle as long as his yacht (221ft); unfortunately there were two inconvenient streams in the way, so it could only be 150ft long. Instead, he had a glass-roofed colonnaded veranda built around three of the sides, along which a piper would play every morning to rouse the guests for breakfast. A magnificent domed conservatory was constructed against the south side, leading from the drawing room to a projecting terrace. Everything had to be of the best. No expense was spared.

The original Conservatory at Kinloch Castle: artist's impression by Martin Howells

Bullough wanted his dream castle to be rose-coloured, so red sandstone was quarried and dressed on the Isle of Arran and shipped the 160 miles by puffer into Loch Scresort; here the boats were unloaded when horses and carts could come alongside at low tide.

For almost three years, an army of 300 workmen from Eigg and Lancashire laboured to build the castle; they were paid an extra shilling a week to wear Rum tartan kilts and, after threatening to strike because of the torment of the Rum midges, smokers were given a bonus of twopence a day 'to keep the midges away'. A squad of master-joiners and wood-turners toiled to complete the elaborate carved woodwork of all the panelling, staircases, balustrades, galleries, bookshelves, furniture and flooring.

Meanwhile, a quarter of a million tons of best Ayrshire top-soil were imported to improve the marshy site and give depth for the establishment of lavish gardens, lawns, a bowling green and a nine-hole golf course, as well as the necessary avenues, roads and paths complete with Japanese-style bridges.

George Bullough also had ambitions to create at Kinloch a sort of boreal Kew Gardens. A huge walled garden was constructed some distance behind the Castle, to the north-west, measuring 350ft (105m) by

The landscaped gardens at Kinloch Castle, before the First World War

194ft (58m). Against the south-facing side of the northern wall, which was 20ft (6 m) high, a series of 14 sectioned hot-houses was built by Halliday of Manchester in which to grow muscatel grapes, figs, peaches and nectarines. On the north-facing side of the wall a series of six domed palm-houses was built, stretching for nearly 200ft (60m). These palm-houses housed humming birds and large heated freshwater tanks in which were kept turtles and small alligators (which eventually escaped and had to be shot because 'they might be interfering with the comfort of the guests'). The palm-houses adjoined a boiler-house and a series of slate-roofed potting sheds and workshops. This huge garden complex was tended by a squad of 12 full-time gardeners led by a head gardener who had been lured from Alton Towers.

In 1899, with the Second Boer War in full swing and Kinloch Castle not yet complete, Bullough refitted the *Rhouma* as a hospital ship and took her to Table Bay in Cape Town, equipped with wards and staffed with teams of doctors and nurses, where she was placed 'at the disposal of the Imperial Authorities for soldiers wounded or invalided from the front line'. The *Rhouma* sailed home in October 1900 with a complement of convalescent soldiers who became the first occupants of the now completed Kinloch Castle. For this act of 'patriotic devotion', George Bullough was knighted in December 1901; he was 31 years old.

Sir George Bullough used Kinloch Castle as a shooting lodge for two or three months a year. It was designed very much as a male preserve where he and his friends could enjoy fishing and stalking and lavish hospitality on a dream island in a dream castle. The maintenance of the estate provided permanent work for dozens of domestic staff, garden-

The Rhouma: oil painting in the Dining room.

ers, gamekeepers, farmhands, tradesmen – and a school-teacher: in all, around 100 souls, based on Kinloch, were dependent on the requirements of the wealthy laird and his island estate.

Kinloch Castle was the Edwardian mansion *par excellence*, with every possible comfort, designed to accommodate the cream of Edwardian society for weeks on end throughout the 'season'. It was equipped with every conceivable new gismo for the turn of the century. The whole house was lit with electricity (Rum was only the second place in Scotland to have electricity – Glasgow was the first), generated by a dynamo in a power-house upstream on the burn behind the castle, from which direct current was brought in via underground cables. There was a small dam in Coire Dubh, up in the hills to the south of the castle, from which a cast-iron pipe dropped 300 metres, giving a high head of water; and the castle had its own steam central heating system throughout, the radiators in elegant marble-topped casings.

There was an internal telephone system (the first in a private residence in Scotland), with a ten-line exchange (Rhum 1) and instruments of brass and rosewood which would all now be collectors' pieces.

And the plumbing! At Kinloch Castle you didn't take a bath *or* a shower – you had both at once. The baths in the four bathrooms have a hooded walnut shower cabinet at one end. These were the last thing in sophisticated Victorian plumbing – an upright jacuzzi, in effect. The baths and floral basins and WCs were made by Shanks of Barrhead, who had exhibited a similar bath at the 1888 Glasgow International Exhibition; that bath had three dials, but the Kinloch baths have two taps and four dials by the side, with seven different functions. Behind

Bath made by Shanks: Kinloch Castle

the wooden facings is an extraordinary array of lead piping bringing hot or cold water, under terrific pressure, to a series of sprays, showers and squirts. The top three dials control the hot or cold water which comes down from above, with settings for a 'shower', a 'douche' (a penetrating deluge from a single opening), a 'wave' (a ribbon of water shooting out at face level) or a 'spray' (needles of water around the sides). Below the waist you can have a 'plunge' (a stream at the level of the knees), a 'sitz' (a shower from the bottom rather than the top) or a 'jet' (a fountain surging up from the centre of the waste outlet!). It was the ultimate bather's dream – and must have been the ultimate plumber's nightmare.

It was to cost George Bullough some £250,000 (£15m in today's terms) to create this temple to private indulgence. Today it is Britain's most intact example of an Edwardian country house. John Betjeman (in *Scotland's Magazine*, December 1959) called Kinloch Castle

> the stone embodiment of good King Edward's reign, a living memorial of the stalking, the fishing and the sailing, the tenantry and plenty of the days before 1914 and the collapse of a world...
>
> There can be few examples surviving in Great Britain of Edwardian splendour equal to the interior of Kinloch Castle... Kinloch Castle remains, an undisturbed example of pre-1914 opulence... In time to come the castle will be a place of pilgrimage for all those who want to see how people lived in good King Edward's days and what was their taste in pictures, colour and furniture.

George and Monica

One of Sir George's circle of friends was a society beauty called Mrs Monica Charrington. She was the eldest daughter of a French aristocrat, Gerard Gustavus Ducarel, 4th Marquis de la Pasture (pronounced *Deláppature*, with the stress on the first 'a'), whose family had fled to England from France in 1791 during the Reign of Terror. Deprived of their lands in France, the de la Pastures were no longer wealthy.

Monique (Monica) Lilly de la Pasture was born in April 1869 in New Zealand, where her father was engaged in a short-lived sheep-farming enterprise; her mother, Léontine Standish, died in childbirth. Monica was raised in England, and grew up to be an outstandingly beautiful young woman. In 1889, at the age of 20, she married Charles Edward Nicholas Charrington, an amiable and wealthy member of the Charrington brewing family and ten years her senior. He was a partner in the family firm, with an imposing country mansion (Frensham Hall, in Surrey) and a town house in Pont Street.

Monica Charrington at the time of her first marriage (1889); detail from a painting by Edward Hughes

He was an accomplished pianist who wrote amateur musicals for performance by his friends, and a passionate cricket enthusiast (he organised a local team based at Frensham Hall).

Charles Charrington and Monica had a daughter, Dorothea Elizabeth, who was born in 1890. The marriage did not last, however: at some time in the next ten years Monica left her husband and her daughter.[1]

I have been unable, alas, to establish the cause or the time of the break-up of the marriage. One family source asserts that she became the lover of a string of gentlemen of wealth and standing, including (at some time) George Bullough. There is no documentary evidence to substantiate this hearsay assumption; but it would be surprising if a woman of Monica's beauty and glamour had not attracted the attention of rich and ardent male suitors.

There is no record of when Monica first met George Bullough; but the Game Book in Kinloch Castle notes that Mrs Monica Charrington and her father, the Marquis de la Pasture, were guests

---

[1] *Charles Charrington, who died in 1936, married twice after his failed marriage to Monica, but had no more children. Dorothea Charrington, who died in 1991 in her 101st year, married three times. Her first husband, Cecil Twining, was killed during the First World War. By her second husband, Alexander Ingleby-Mackenzie, she had a son, Angus Mackenzie-Charrington (b. 1918), and by her third husband, Robert Bonham Christie, she had a daughter, Yolande, known as 'Pips'. Dorothea always strove to bring the two sides of the family together, and Angus and Pips were encouraged to regard Rum as a special family place: Pips has fished on Rum on a number of occasions, and Angus used Kinloch Castle to celebrate his son's 50th birthday in 1995. Angus met his grandmother Monica – 'the grand-mère' – a few times, but always in formal circumstances and, despite all Dorothea's efforts, relations with her mother always remained somewhat distant.*

The Hall of Kinloch Castle
-The Gallery of the Castle Hall

on a shooting party there in October 1902.

Sir George (as he was then) was cited as the co-respondent in the Charrington divorce. The decree nisi was granted in November, 1902, and made absolute on 15 May, 1903. Just over a month later, on 24 June, 1903, Sir George and Monica were married in a glittering society wedding at Kinloch Castle. George was 33 years old, Monica a year older. They had only one child, a daughter, Hermione, who was born in November 1906. [1]

Whether or not she had 'lost her name', as the phrase went in those days, Monica's marriage to Sir George Bullough offered the opportunity to get back into 'Society' – and that is what she seems to have set out to do, with single-minded determination (see below, *Edwardian heyday*). The marriage also heralded a new era for the Castle. Monica's arrival as chatelaine brought about a marked transformation in what had been designed as the equivalent of London gentlemen's club. She commandeered the sunniest rooms on the ground floor of the Castle for her own quarters, and provided a feminity of touch and an elegance of taste in what had been an exclusively masculine domain. She also instigated extensive building works which added a second floor of guest bedrooms on the west side of the Castle.

Inside the Castle

It is now some 80 years since Kinloch Castle was fully occupied, yet its furnishings are intact, its style quite unchanged.

A visitor's first impression on entering the Castle up the shallow balustraded steps is one of overwhelming opulence and extravagance.

The galleried Hall was intended to impress: and impress it still does. This is the heart of the house. It is lit by three huge mullioned window bays at first storey height, draped with plush curtains frogged in gold braid like military saddle-cloths. Heavily-antlered stags' heads gaze glassy-eyed from the walls. There are tigerskin rugs on the polished floor, a black Steinway concert grand piano made in 1900, and a clutter of exotic furniture – Cairene tables, Japanese lacquer cabinets, Indi-

[1] *I have heard it suggested that Monica may have been one of the Prince of Wales' many mistresses, and that Sir George Bullough was persuaded to 'take on' Monica to avoid the scandal of Royal involvement in a divorce suit; his knighthood in 1901 is alleged, by inference, to have been a reward for this delicate private service rather than for his public services to the Crown during the Boer War. It's an intriguing possibility, obviously; but there is no mention whatsoever of Monica, or George Bullough, or of Rum, in all the extensive literature about Edward VII; nor have I been able to find any evidence that Edward's handsome racing yacht, the Britannia, was ever berthed anywhere in the Western Isles.*

an brass-stopped tables, brocaded and tasselled sofas and triangular bobbin-turned chairs. Two huge Japanese bronze incense burners, 11ft tall, flank the arcade into the corridor; surmounted by an eagle fighting a dragon, each vase is supported on a tongue of flame from a dragon base and gripped by griffin handles.[1]

Monica Bullough at 40: painting by Hugh Rivière, now in the Hall of the Castle

Another massive piece is a bronze of a giant Japanese monkey-eating eagle on a tree stump hunting monkeys.[2]

There are two larger-than-life full-length portraits of Monica and George, painted by Hugh Rivière[3] in 1909 and 1910, to celebrate their respective 40th birthdays: she elegant in evening gown and very beautiful, he handsome and kilted.

In a large recess under the neo-Jacobean staircase is a mechanical automatic orchestra called the Orchestrion – the Edwardian equivalent of a juke-box. It is basically a sophisticated electrically-driven barrel-organ with several ranks of tubular or trumpet-shaped pipes and percussion accompaniment – various drums, a cymbal and a triangle. It creates a full 40-piece orchestral effect through large perforated rolls of paper (and some of paper-thin brass), playing everything from Wagner (*Lohengrin*) and selections from *Faust* and *Coppelia* to military marches and contemporary 'pop' songs like *The Honeysuckle and the Bee, Ma Blushin' Rosie* and *Home, Sweet Home*. A collection of 38 original

[1] *These were a gift from the Emperor of Japan, in gratitude for Sir George's services during the Russo-Japanese War; the peace treaty was signed on the Rhouma.*

[2] *There was also a superb figure of an eagle in carved ivory, standing 30 inches high and with a wingspan of about three feet, one of a pair of sculptures by the Japanese artist Nuirikuni Otake; it is said to be the most valuable piece in the Kinloch collection. One of the pair was bought by the Emperor of Japan at an auction in Yokohama as a wedding present for the Tsar of Russia's niece; the other was bought at the same auction by George Bullough. The Russian eagle is in the Kremlin's Armoury Museum; the Bullough eagle is on display in the Ivy Wu Gallery of the National Museum of Scotland in Chambers Street, Edinburgh. The wooden tree-stump base for the ivory eagle is in the rear (courtyard) entrance lobby in Kinloch Castle. Another fine piece from the Castle on display in the Ivy Wu Gallery is a 19th century Japanese bronze group of a cock standing on a tree-stump looking down at a hen and three chicks. The detail is remarkable, with swirling lava-like rocks, small petalled flowers, blossoms and rocks.*

[3] *Hugh Goldwin Rivière (1869-1956) was an established portrait painter who had exhibited at the Royal Academy in 1890. He was the son of Briton Rivière (1840-1926), a well-known painter of animals and also portraits of people, often with their own favourite animals.*

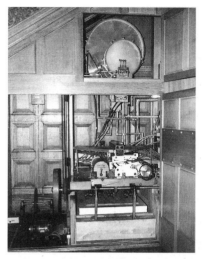

The Orchestrion

music rolls survives, like the Orchestrion, all in perfect working order. Sir George installed it in 1906 for £2,000 (£120,000 in today's terms) but, because it had been designed for somewhere else, the pipes had to be adapted and the woodwork altered to allow it to fit under the staircase. It still booms out military marches and polkas and operatic highlights to the delight of visitors, heralded by a clatter of belts and pulleys and a series of whirrings and wheezes before the music begins. [1]

The gallery which encircles three sides of the Hall is lined with a series of large Rum landscapes commissioned by Sir George from the Manchester painter Byron Cooper (1850-1933) between 1900 and 1902; several Cooper watercolours are to be found in other rooms. The gallery also contains, among other *objets d'art*, a handsome pair of 7ft plum-coloured *cloisonné* vases (another gift from the Emperor of Japan), and much Japanese furniture inlaid with ivory and mother-of-pearl.

The Dining Room, panelled with lozenges of polished mahogany, looks out over Loch Scresort. Over the mantelpiece hangs a portrait of Sir George's father, John Bullough; there is also a Gainsborough-style portrait of his son George at the age of 16. An oil painting of the *Rhouma* at sea, brigantine-rigged, hangs on another wall. The oval table is set with lead crystal candelabra with elegant bell-shaped Cricklite smoke-shades on press-moulded bases, imitating cut-glass. The heavy mahogany Chippendale-style dining chairs came from the staterooms of the *Rhouma*: a stretcher across the bottom has a hole by which the chair could be bolted to the floor, and the tops swivel. The electric lights are in the form of Japanese incense burners flanked by dragons. [2]

The Ballroom was specifically designed to be just that, with a well sprung oak floor and a galaxy of star-like twinkling lights in the lofty barrel ceiling. There is a musicians' gallery, which was used by the orchestra from the *Rhouma* for dances, with a pile of abandoned instruments in a corner. The wall-hangings are silk, the chandelier crystal. The furniture around the walls is rather special. The silk damask of the deep-

---

[1] *The Orchestrion was manufactured by Imhof & Mukle of Vöhrenbach in Baden, whose New Oxford Street salon proclaimed itself to be 'By Appointment to the late Queen Victoria'. Only three of this model were made; this one may have been ordered for Balmoral Castle by Queen Victoria, who died before it was ready to be installed.*

[2] *Originally the walls were hung with a set of handsome 17th century Flemish tapestries from Brussels, 9ft by 15ft, now stored in the National Museum of Scotland. They depict 'The Healing of the Lame Beggar', 'The Angel releasing St Peter from Prison' and 'Tobias taking leave of his blind father, Tobit' (from the Apocrypha).*

buttoned sofas, which have seldom had their original chintz covers removed, is still a brilliant gold. It was a room for very private party-ing: the windows were deliberately set at such a height that no one could see in from the courtyard, and drinks were served through a hatch in the panelling from the butler's pantry.

The Billiard Room was the heart of the masculine domain of Sir George's castle, complete with its club fender, leather armchairs and vel-vet curtains. It has a 'Eureka' table with 'Extra Low Fast Cushion' from Burroughes & Watts of Soho Square; the room has a dais from which the game can be watched, and also an ample sitting area for non-play-ers. One ingenious feature of the room, which faces into the cold central courtyard, is the double-glazing system for the windows: the two panes open together in parallel on a Z-frame. Vents to get rid of the cigar-smoke were concealed behind the parapet of the panelling; fresh air was pumped in through a metal grill in the floor under the billiard table.

The Library was formerly George's business room in the south-west corner, at the end of the corridor by the sportsmen's entrance. The 2,000 books are a careful collection of literary yarns and books on court etiquette, French nobility, Guards history and sporting pursuits (including the Racing Calendar from 1914 to 1929, and a complete set of *Bai-ley's Magazine*, the gentleman's sporting chronicle of its day), a set

Napoleon explaining to Pope Pius VII the plans for his coronation as Emperor in 1804

of 1888 encyclopaedias, and some mild Victorian pornography.

There is also a set of 20 leather-bound photograph albums, each gold-embossed with the names of the places the Bulloughs had visited in their world travels: Australia, Burma, California, Ceylon, China (in 1894), Honolulu, India (6 volumes), New Caledonia, New Zealand, Salt Lake City and South Africa, plus a volume called Natives of the World. They are for the most part undated, but appear to cover many years, starting long before the Bullough marriage. They are a motley collec-tion, and include rather gruesome photographs of beheadings in the Boxer Rebellion and the crucifixion of dacoits in Burma. Some of the pictures were taken at the time by their private photographer; others look like commercial postcards bought on the spot.

Lady Monica's Drawing Room in the south-eastern corner of the Castle is the feminine heart of the house. Lady Bullough transformed it into an elegant parlour for her own use, decorated in an Edwardian pastel version of the Adam style, with white moulded ceiling and hand-embroidered silk wall-hangings and Adamesque fireplaces, one of them set in a deep inglenook. A pilastered arch enlarged it to include the room next door. The carpet is olive, the chairs and chaise-longues covered with glazed chintz, the tables inlaid with enamelled white and gilt. Against one wall stands a one-handed clock.

The Empire Room, next to the Drawing Room, was formerly the library or morning room, and this, too, Lady Bullough converted into a private retreat, decorated in gold, white and red. She called it the 'Empire Room' because she claimed descent (however tenuous) from one of Napoleon's younger sisters, Caroline (Maria Annunziata, 1782-1839); in 1800 Caroline married Joachim Murat, an inn-keeper's son from Gascony who had become a general in the French army and was later appointed King of Naples. A portrait of Napoleon hangs on one of the walls, and above the fireplace there is a large engraving of Napoleon explaining to Pope Pius VII the plans for his coronation as Emperor in 1804. The furniture in the room is fashionably neo-classical, and the silk lamp-shades are original (they probably survived because the power-supply was so weak that they never got singed).

Lady Monica's Bedroom upstairs is the one room which isn't 'genuine'. It is situated at the south-east corner of the Castle, and the turret suffered a lot of damage during the years the Castle was locked up, so the room had to be replastered and redecorated. It now feels curiously ordinary compared with the rest of the Castle. Next door to it is *Sir George's Bedroom,* which in fact used to be Lady Bullough's dressing room (Sir George occupied a suite of private apartments elsewhere). It now contains a handsome bed of inlaid mahogany with a tall crown of fragile drapes and fraying tassels; the walls are hung with prints of Harrow. There is a full-length oval swivelling dressing-mirror and a small Japanese writing desk. On the hearth his knee-boots stand ready for wear, the boot-trees engraved with his name; an antiquated weighing machine occupies one corner. The spirit of the Bulloughs still inhabits every corner of Kinloch Castle.

Edwardian heyday

The decade before the outbreak of the first World War was the heyday of the Edwardian Age – and of the Rum of Kinloch Castle.

It was during this decade that Lady Bullough began to show her steely determination to achieve high social standing; this centred almost exclusively on her second daughter, Hermione, at the expense of her daughter from her first marriage, Dorothea Charrington. The Bulloughs already had a London town house in Connaught Place, as well as the island resort of Rum. Not long after the marriage Monica persuaded her husband to buy a place in Herefordshire, Bishopwood House at Ledbury, where Sir George became Master of the Fox Hounds in 1908 (a position he held until 1922). To be MFH was a big step up on the landed gentry ladder.

The next stage of the game plan to get into Edwardian society was to live at Newmarket, because racing provided the real entrée to the society of King Edward VII's time: racing society then was somewhat 'looser' and certainly more tolerant of foibles and past peccadilloes than Victorian society had been – at Newmarket anything went, as long as you were winning races. Sir George bought two studs, and placed his horses with the King's trainer with considerable success;

Pony-stalking in 1901: head stalker Duncan McNaughton (with pipe) and Jimmy McAskill

he won the 'Wartime' Grand National at Gatwick with Ballymacad in 1917 (two of Ballymacad's shoes are mounted and displayed in the Library), the Gold Cup and the Golden Vase at Ascot with Golden Myth in 1922, and the 1,000 Guineas with Campanula in 1934. In 1922 he built himself a large house at Newmarket, called Warren Hill, and in the same year came the ultimate social accolade: Sir George was elected to the Jockey Club.

Life for the Bulloughs was an idyll of purposeful idleness. At Newmarket Sir George would eat a huge breakfast every morning and play a round of golf, skip lunch, visit his stables, and then dine formally in the evening. This was his regular routine, broken only by visits to other stately homes and the autumn visit to Rum for the shooting season.

Everything had been done to make Rum a rural version of Belgravia. The roads had been improved beyond recognition (the estate employed 14 full-time roadmen). This was to improve access to Kilmory, where the Castle's laundry had been built (it is now a rusting shell of corrugated iron, with pieces of the original stove lying in a pile outside), and to the shooting lodge at Harris. The Bulloughs imported two luxurious horse-drawn carriages, with deep blue upholstery and the Bullough monograph on the door-panels. Unfortunately the two horses were unable to pull them up the 'Big Brae' beyond Kinloch; and since this was the only road on the island apart from those round the Castle, there was nowhere else for them to go. The handsome carriages were never used again, and mouldered to pieces in a shed.

The transport situation on Rum was dramatically improved when the Bulloughs imported two gleaming sports cars – Albions, built in Glasgow – in which Sir George and his guests would indulge in races to Harris (it's said they could do 60 miles an hour!). It was claimed that the roads were in such good condition that the cars could make the hilly, twisty five-mile journey to Kilmory in five minutes dead, but it sounds very unlikely.

The late-summer visits to Rum were relatively brief, but regular as clockwork. Everything was geared to make life as effortless and comfortable as possible. Archie Cameron, who was born on Rum in 1903 and wrote a delightful account of his boyhood there (*Bare Feet and Tackety Boots*, 1988), has left us with a graphic description of life under the Bulloughs.

For months in advance, estate staff would have been labouring to prepare for their arrival. The roads which Sir George had built to Kilmory and Harris were repaired, sanded and raked to ensure ease of passage for the two Albions. Fresh ponies were broken in, to be ready for work on the deer stalks. Boats were taken on carts to some of the lochs in the hills for fishing expeditions. Palms, plants and flowers were brought in from the hot-houses to decorate the hall and rooms of the Castle.

As the *Rhouma* nosed into Loch Scresort, the mechanics and chauffeurs would be drawn up with the Albions, ready to fetch the guests from the pier. The four ghillies and gamekeepers would be dressed in their new issues of Rum tweed. The kitchens, usually under the rule of mercurial French chefs, would be a-fever with activity. The whole island came alive, and stayed alive for the weeks of 'the season'.

When the Bulloughs were in residence the *Rhouma* was moored in the bay, and the band would come ashore to play in the Ballroom's minstrels' gallery.

Among the guests were numbered a troupe of Gaiety girls, friends of Lily Elsie, the musical comedy actress, wife of Sir George's half-brother, Major Ian Bullough. Every morning the head stalker, Duncan McNaughton (whose son George became Warden for the Nature Conservancy in 1957, see CHAPTER 7), would rouse the Castle occupants with his bagpipes, marching along the colonnaded terrace at the stroke of 8 o'clock.

The highlight and culmination of the season, for the islanders, were the Rum Highland Games; these had all the events associated with traditional Highland Games, with some of the guests (particularly Sir George's army friends) taking part. There was beer on tap all day. There were three tug-of-war teams: one from the *Rhouma*, one from the gardeners, and one from the farmworkers, ghillies and gamekeepers (the last invariably won).

Shooting Party at Kinloch Castle

It was a golden period, and Archie Cameron remembers it with unalloyed pleasure:

> The Castle and its occupants were to us the centre of the universe. Sir George and his lady were the most kindly and courteous people... I have nothing but very pleasant memories of that gracious lady.

End of an era

As the glittering pre-war Edwardian era began to draw to a close, so the clouds began to gather over Kinloch Castle.

The pleasures of luxury sailing lost their appeal. In 1903 Sir George had bought a new 43-ft wood-screw steamer of 18 tons which he named the *Kinloch* and which he soon replaced with *Kinloch II* (formerly the *Magnificent*), a much larger wood-screw ketch of 108 tonnes and 80-ft overall. In 1911, however, Sir George sold the *Rhouma*.[1]

In her place he bought a steel twin-screw sloop called the *Triton*, which he renamed the *Rhouma II*. She was a rather more modest vessel, 170ft long overall and 318 tons, which had been built in 1902 by the Ailsa ship-building company of Troon. Sir George sold her (and *Kinloch II*) in 1919, when he appears to have 'swallowed the anchor' and given up sailing.[2]

---

[1] *The Rhouma was commissioned into the Italian Navy in July 1912 as an armed yacht and renamed the Giuliana. Her overall length was slightly increased and her gross tonnage raised from 670 to 934; she was eventually decommissioned in 1928.*

[2] *Rhouma II had a series of owners (and names) after she was sold by Sir George Bullough. She was owned by W. D. Wills from 1934-38 (the Wills family also bought the estate of Meggernie, in Perthshire, which Sir George's father, John Bullough, had once owned). She ended her days in 1975, registered in Panama under the name Madiz.*

Hermione Bullough (Countess of Durham) as a young girl; detail from a portrait by Sidney W White

The outbreak of war in 1914 changed the island's life-style radically. The 40 able-bodied men of the outdoor staff were mounted on ponies, drilled on the lawn, and sent off to the trenches, from which only two returned to Rum. Sir George, who had served as a captain in the Scottish Horse Imperial Yeomanry from 1908-11, was appointed Superintendent of the Remount Department with the rank of major. The Castle was put on to a care and maintenance basis. The *Rhouma II* was given over to minesweeping duties. In 1915 Sir George relinquished his military position, and in 1916 he was elevated to the baronetcy 'for his services to the nation', after having publicly loaned £50,000 to the Government at no interest (£2.5m today).

After the war, attitudes to the frivolous life-styles of the Edwardian era changed beyond recognition. An era had ended, not only for Europe but for Rum. The Castle was never to be the same again. Although the family affection for it remained, the visits to Rum became less and less frequent and eventually all but petered out. Bereft of the life-giving injections of regular occupation, and the constant care of a large resident staff, the dream castle at Kinloch began its slow decline. The heating in the conservatory and the palm-houses failed, and the humming-birds died, to be stuffed by a taxidermist in London and mounted as ornaments in the Castle. The fountain in the front lawn ran dry. The lawns and manicured bowling greens grew rank and unkempt.

The elaborate gardens became overgrown. The exotic glass-houses decayed. There is not a great deal left to see of the garden complex now. It is mostly covered with scrub, in the midst of which the original long wall still survives, as well as the collapsed wooden remains of some of the hot-houses on the south side. On the north side of the wall only the foundation outlines of the palm-houses and the heated tanks with their underground pipes can still be discerned.

The population of the island, which had numbered 53 souls in 1891 when George Bullough inherited it, had risen to more than 100 by 1900. By 1932 this figure had declined to 32, however, and by 1951 to 28. The sheep which had been grazed on Rum for a century were all gone by 1926, although Lady Bullough would let the grazing again during the Second World War. Once again, Rum was virtually the deserted island.

Family aftermath

The Bulloughs' daughter, Hermione, had been a pale and sickly child. She grew up to be tall and delicate-looking, according to Archie Campbell; he recalls that a white nanny goat was specially imported to Rum to provide the right kind of milk for her. She was presented at court in 1926 at the age of 20 (rather later than was customary); it was the fulfilment of Monica Bullough's desire to be accepted in society. In 1931, at the age of 25, Hermione married the 5th Earl of Durham, a 46-year-old widower – the final feather in Monica's cap.[1]

Hermione Bullough and the 5th Earl of Durham had a son, the Hon. John George Lambton, who was born in June 1932; he visited Rum at least once before the war, in 1938, and he celebrated his 21st birthday at Kinloch Castle with a glittering party in 1953. His mother, Hermione, the Countess of Durham, died in 1992.

Exit the Bulloughs

Sir George Bullough died from a heart attack while playing golf on holiday in the Pas de Calais, Boulogne, in July, 1939, at the age of 69. His obituary in *The Times* barely mentioned Rum, but concentrated on his life as a racehorse owner, breeder and turf administrator. It said of him '...he devoted himself to developing sport on the best lines... He possessed an equable temperament and took a calm and humane view of life.' His remains were brought from France to Rum for interment in the mausoleum, in a huge pink granite sarcophagus beside the tomb of his father.

Sir George was still a wealthy man at the time of his death. In his will he left just over £700,000. To his wife he left £25,000 and all his goods and chattels, the use of the family homes, and the income from the 'residual estate'; everything would go to his daughter Hermione after Lady Bullough's death.

The whole estate, including Rum, passed into the hands of Trustees. The will stipulated that 'if my Trustees shall at any time consider that the income of my wife is insufficient to enable her... to maintain in a proper state the Isle of Rhum and my residence there I empower them... to raise it out of the capital of my residual estate.'

After Sir George's death, Lady Bullough continued to live at War-

[1] *The Earl of Durham's first wife, whom he married in 1919, had died in 1924, having borne him two sons: John Roderick (Viscount Lambton), who shot himself in 1941, and Antony, who succeeded his brother as Viscount Lambton and was Conservative MP for Berwick-upon-Tweed from 1951-73. When his father died in 1970 at the age of 85, Viscount Lambton renounced the earldom in order to stay in the House of Commons, but was allowed to keep the courtesy title of Viscount. Lord Lambton now spends much of his time in Italy; one of his daughters is Lucinda Lambton, the writer, photographer and television presenter*

ren Hill, Newmarket, for the next three decades; she also bought (perhaps for sentimental reasons) the small Chateau de Courset in Normandy which had been the de la Pasture ancestral home. She still made occasional visits to Rum to join shooting parties; her last visit was in 1954, at the age of 85, when, despite failing eyesight, she drove an old Austin car on a sentimental journey over the boulder-strewn tracks to the Bullough Mausoleum at Harris.

According to family sources, Lady Bullough is thought to have offered the island to the Queen, who had landed on 'the Forbidden Isle' for secluded family picnics on Kilmory beach during Hebridean voyages on the new royal yacht, *Britannia*. The Royal Family, however, had no need for Rum as a holiday home in Scotland when they already had Balmoral Castle.

Be that as it may, in 1957, on February 28 (the date of Sir George Bullough's birthday), the Bullough Trustees sold Rum to the Nature Conservancy for £23,000 (see CHAPTER 7). Lady Bullough was insistent that she herself should be buried on Rum in due course, and some panels of reinforced concrete were obtained to keep on stand-by for a temporary sarcophagus at short notice. Ten years later, in June 1967, at the ripe old age of 98, Lady Bullough was taken back to Rum and her final resting place. She had died on May 22. On June 6 – a characteristically wet and windy day – her coffin was driven to Harris over the bumpy road in the back of a Nature Conservancy Land Rover attended by two undertakers who had brought her from Newmarket. After a service of committal by the Episcopalian minister in Fort William (Rev George Henderson, later the Bishop of Argyll and the Isles) she was placed in the concrete tomb which had been assembled in the Bullough mausoleum, to lie alongside her father-in-law and her husband. Six months later the sarcophagus was encased in slabs of polished granite.

The mausoleum was not included in the sale of the island to the Nature Conservancy; it remains in the hands of the Bullough trustees, and Sir George's descendants have perpetual access to it. It is a striking epitaph to a chapter of extravagant opulence in the island's story.

CHAPTER 7

A National Nature Reserve

> Rum is an island which has been put to work, to effect not only its own salvation but also that of other islands and the vast tracts of the mainland which are also suffering from degraded bioproductivity.

THAT WAS THE PHILOSOPHY which informed the decision by the Nature Conservancy to take on the challenge of Rum in 1957 and designate it as a National Nature Reserve (NNR). Since then it has been wholly owned and managed by government conservation agencies – the Nature Conservancy (1957-73), the Nature Conservancy Council (1973-91), the Nature Conservancy Council for Scotland (1991-92) and now, since 1992, Scottish Natural Heritage.

What is an NNR?

Scotland now has 70 National Nature Reserves, which form a series of key sites which are nationally or internationally important for their 'biological, geological or physiographical features'. They represent some of the least disturbed and therefore most important areas of natural or semi-natural vegetation in this country; in natural heritage terms they are outstanding locations for their diversity of wildlife and landscape. But how did NNRs come about?

In 1949, the Scottish Wildlife Conservation Special Committee, chaired by James Ritchie, produced a Report to Parliament entitled *Nature Reserves in Scotland* (Command 7814). This report, which chimed with a 1947 report by a committee for England and Wales chaired by Sir Julian Huxley, recommended the setting-up of nature reserves in which the 'principal or dominant land-use' should be nature conservation:

> By nature reserves we understand areas delimited for the express purpose of safeguarding and perpetuating the natural assemblages of plants and animals which they now contain, plant and animal assemblages which might settle there under more favourable conditions, and special features of geological interest.

This echoed the Huxley Report definition for a nature reserve:

> ...a tract of country, the existing character of which it is desired to preserve as far as possible, either for the singular beauty of its landscape or for its scientific value, or more usually for a combination of both.

The Huxley Report proposed the 'setting aside' of 73 reserves in England and Wales; the Ritchie Report recommended 50 reserves for

Scotland. One of the 50 sites envisaged for future 'setting aside' was 'the island of Rhum' (which was then still in the ownership of the Bullough family):

> Rhum, one of the larger islands of the Inner Hebridean Group, contains numerous valleys, streams and lochs; its jagged peaks reach a height of 2,659ft (810 m). Most of the island is deer forest; there is little woodland and little cultivation, for the total human population is under twenty. Its flora and fauna are of much scientific interest. It has fine cliffs for sea birds, one species of which, the Manx shearwater, breeds high up in the hills.
>
> Isolated, yet within easy reach of the mainland, it would make an outstanding station for research and experiment, and indeed is the most suitable island for this purpose in Scotland.

The National Parks and Access to the Countryside Act 1949 empowered the newly-founded Nature Conservancy 'to establish, maintain and manage' nature reserves; such nature reserves were to be managed for the protection of features of outstanding nature conservation interest and for the specific purpose of study and research. The Act introduced the 'key site' philosophy as a central tenet of nature conservation in Britain; this philosophy, strengthened by statute in 1981, underlies the system of Sites of Special Scientific Interest (SSSIs) in England, Scotland and Wales.

Two years after the Act was passed, in 1951, the first National Nature Reserve in Britain was declared, at Beinn Eighe in the north-west Highlands. Six years later, Rum was added to the portfolio.

The purchase of Rum

In 1956, word was circulating in environmental circles that the island of Rum might be coming on the market. Rum had for a long time been on the Nature Conservancy's 'hit-list' for possible acquisition as a self-contained nature reserve, and Max Nicholson, Director-General of the Nature Conservancy and one of the most formidable and effective figures in 20th century environmental politics in Britain, wrote to Lady Bullough requesting a meeting. He met her at her home in Newmarket to try to persuade her to transfer ownership to an organisation which would ensure the island's future for all time.

He was delighted to find that he was pushing at an open door. Lady Bullough was already determined to secure the future of Rum: she was concerned that her daughter, Hermione, the dowager Countess of Durham (see CHAPTER 6), would simply want to dispose of it to the highest bidder. She wanted, above all, that it should go to 'the right owner'.

Max Nicholson and Lady Bullough hit it off at once: 'she was a wonderfully charming person, still elegant and beautiful at the age of nearly 90, strong-willed but with a core of sound common sense', he says. She obviously cared about the island a great deal, and not simply for sentimental reasons. They met half a dozen times at Newmarket while the negotiations proceeded; they reminisced a lot about the old times on Rum, and became firm friends.

The question of price was never a problem: Lady Bullough agreed to accept whatever price the official District Valuer placed upon it. So in February 1957 the island of Rum was formally bought from the Trustees of the late Sir George Bullough by the Nature Conservancy for the sum of £23,000. It was a remarkable bargain, considering that John Bullough had paid £35,000 for it in 1888!

The Nature Conservancy acquired Rum lock, stock and barrel. In a Minute of Agreement between 'Dame Monica Lilly Bullough and the Nature Conservancy', Lady Bullough also made a gift to the Nature Conservancy of 'the whole furnishings and plenishings within Kinloch Castle', apart from a number of *objets d'art* which were to be given to the Royal Scottish Museum in Edinburgh. The gift was to be known as The Sir George Bullough Memorial. She expressed the wish that the Castle should be kept as it had been in its Edwardian heyday. The only exception to the sale of the island was the Bullough Mausoleum at Harris, which was retained by the Trustees and was to be used only as a burial place for Lady Bullough and the descendants of Sir George Bullough 'and for no other purposes'.

Central Rum landscape

The Nature Conservancy 'agreed that it would (unless prevented from doing so by circumstances over which it had no control) use the island for the purpose of a Nature Reserve in perpetuity, and maintain Kinloch Castle and the adjacent premises thereon (so far as it might be practicable to do so in the circumstances)'.

Rum was declared a National Nature Reserve in April 1957. The Designation Statement said:

> Never having been a tourist or mountaineering resort, and having no crofters, the island is ideally suited for much field research which it has been impossible to undertake elsewhere owing to disturbance. For example, deer movements and habits cannot be scientifically studied if the deer are liable to indiscriminate disturbance, nor can the effects of

grazing and burning on vegetation be investigated where uncontrolled livestock and fires are liable to upset the experiments.

Restoration of the natural vegetation including native trees is also included in the Conservancy's programme and should be less difficult than in other parts of the Highlands and Islands owing to the care taken of the Island by the late Sir George Bullough and his family, who have long kept it free from disturbance while giving facilities for scientific studies.

Getting to work

The Trustees had stipulated that the estate staff permanently resident on the island should be offered employment by the Nature Conservancy on terms and conditions not less advantageous than those they currently enjoyed. And that created the first problem for the Nature Conservancy.

At that time the sheep-grazing on the island was let by the estate to a farmer in Easter Ross, who kept 1750 sheep and 40 cattle on the island, and used it as a holiday resort (he would stay at the White House for summer holidays with his family). He employed three shepherds, at Kilmory, Harris and Kinloch. The Nature Conservancy had no place for sheep in its plans. Something had to give.

John Arbuthnott, who would later succeed his father as the Viscount of Arbuthnott and become chairman of the Scottish Advisory Committee of the NCC (1980-85), was the Nature Conservancy's Land Agent for Scotland at the time. He recalls the difficult negotiations with the farmer over the removal of his sheep. The farmer had already ended his lease from Lady Bullough, but now hoped to sell all his sheep to the Nature Conservancy, and tended to negotiate with a bottle of whisky in one hand and a club in the other. He appealed to the Secretary of State for Scotland to over-ride the Nature Conservancy's decision; Max Nicholson now stepped in and reminded The Scottish Office that this was none of its business – it was a strictly management matter. There was no legal obligation on the Nature Conservancy to renew the lease, and the sheep and cattle were eventually removed, much to the farmer's annoyance – 'the second Rum Clearances', as the popular press called it. The three shepherds left with the sheep.

When the Nature Conservancy acquired Rum, the island was in a state of suspended animation. The estate manager was the former head stalker, Duncan McNaughton, who had been on Rum since 1913; his son George was now the head stalker. The island was let to shooting parties in the autumn – mainly for stalking, because there were very few red grouse left. Kinloch Castle was on a minimal care-and-maintenance basis for most of the year, run by two caretakers, Mr and Mrs Wilson. The home farm was still in operation: it was run primarily to provide

The school in 1958: Mrs Isla Stewart with her 14 pupils

fresh milk and potatoes for the community, and a supply of hay, some grazing and unthreshed corn for the farm stock and the pony stud. It derived a little income from the sale of ponies, foals, calves and other stock, and a few potatoes. The ponies were vital for the autumn deer cull.

When the Nature Conservancy took over, the personnel changed to some extent. The caretaker of the Castle was on the mainland, ill, and he and his wife decided not to stay on; a new caretaker was appointed, Captain Hamish Gordon (who had been the harbourmaster in Karachi), with his wife as housekeeper. But the key players remained. Duncan McNaughton retired as estate manager, and was succeeded by his son George, who was now given the title of Warden of the NNR; he had known Rum since boyhood, which was an enormous help in managing the island. George McNaughton provided the backbone of the Reserve: a skilled aero-engine mechanic from his RAF service, an experienced tradesman, a gamekeeper, gardener, stockman andcoxswain. Taciturn, unassuming and ubiquitous, he enjoyed high standing in the Rum community; in 1973 he would be appointed to the new post of Chief Warden, before moving on to the Muir of Dinnet National Nature Reserve in his final years with the Nature Conservancy Council.

The home farm stockman, Jimmy Smith, remained on Rum at the

Nature Conservancy take-over, as did three estate workers: Jimmy's brother, John; Hugh Boland, a former coal-miner from Muirkirk in Ayrshire; and Harry Stewart, who was married to the schoolteacher, Mrs Isla Stewart. There was also a ferryman/handyman, Donald Park, who was a retired seaman from Scalpay, Harris.

The schoolteacher was a newcomer. Her predecessor had been married to one of the shepherds, who had declined a job as an estate worker for the Nature Conservancy and had gone to the mainland with his wife.

The island sub-postmistress was Jessie Smith, sister of Jimmy and John; she had come to Rum from Arisaig as a child in 1938, when her father, John, a forester who had worked on the Rothiemurchus estate, had been appointed stockman on the Kinloch farm.

It was a thriving, busy, close-knit community. There were ten children in the primary school. And the community had its own grandparents living there: Duncan McNaughton stayed on after retirement, and lived in Lion Cottage, and John Smith senior stayed as well, and lived with his unmarried son, Jimmy.

Although they all had their designated jobs, they all helped one another when required: Jimmy Smith was helped on the farm by one or two of the estate workers; Donald Park, the ferryman/handyman, had Harry Stewart to help with the boat and the distribution of mail and cargoes; George McNaughton as Warden had call on everyone for stalking and routine work on the estate. When occasion demanded, the whole island joined in – for instance, for the annual visit of the puffer with the coal supplies, which had to be unloaded between tides.

As John Arbuthnott recalls, 'We had a duty to the resident community no less than to nature conservation, and we took both responsibilities very seriously. We needed them just as much as they needed us.'

Warden/Naturalist

The Nature Conservancy's Conservation Officer (Scotland) was the late Joe Eggeling, who would later succeed John Berry as Director in Scotland. Joe had worked in Uganda as Chief Conservator of Forests, and right from the start he saw the purchase of the island as a unique opportunity to re-create natural-type Hebridean woodland on Rum and thereby restore its biological productivity and diversify its plant and animal species.

The first task for the Nature Conservancy was to appoint a Warden/Naturalist for the island. The job went to a 27-year-old forester from Lincolnshire called Peter Wormell, who would remain as Warden/Naturalist until 1973 – 16 crucial years in the story of the island.

Peter had just come home on leave after a three-year stint working in Northern Rhodesia with a survey team which was engaged in mapping the forest cover of the country. He saw the Nature Conservancy's advertisement for the post on Rum, and applied; he was appointed on the strength of his forestry experience and went up to Edinburgh at the beginning of June 1957 for a crash course on the Nature Conservancy's work and its reserves in Scotland.

In early July he set foot on Rum for the first time. It was a difficult and delicate role for a 27-year-old. Peter was, in effect, taking over the role of laird from the Bulloughs, and the islanders, all of whom had been estate workers under the Bulloughs, were convinced that he had come to evict them. His standing among the locals was considerably enhanced when he started courting Jessie Smith, the postmistress; they married in May, 1958. His father-in-law, John Smith, with his wealth of forestry experience, was a tremendous help to Peter in his work.

Joe Eggeling, with the help of Peter Wormell and John Arbuthnott, prepared the first Management Plan for Rum in 1959, which indicated the immediate priorities:

> The primary object of management must be research directed at recreating the natural characteristics of a Hebridean island so that Rhum may be restored to the highest level of biological productivity that can be sustained naturally, measured in terms of population levels and species composition of the appropriate flora and fauna. This will involve... the measurement of the effects of different practices of land utilisation, supported by experiment to discover how best to improve fertility and obtain the maximum long-term biological yield from the soil.
>
> Diversification of the habitat by the re-establishment of scrub or woodland cover, and also by the provision of more conventional plantations and shelter-belts, by methods which may include draining and the use of mineral fertilisers, must take a high place in the programme.
>
> Secondary objects of management include:
>
> (i) the safeguarding of flora and fauna of special interest, e.g. the arctic-alpine vegetation, and the Manx shearwater colonies of the mountain tops; and
> (ii) subject to Government approval in due course, the establishment of a Field Studies Centre based on the Castle, with facilities for demonstration, education and research...

In the Conclusion, the Plan had no doubt about the importance of the Rum community:

> The essential requirement underlying all estate management on Rhum is the absolute necessity of maintaining a thriving and contented community. This need has to be borne in mind whenever any decision is taken. It governs the selection of staff, the allocation of their duties and above all the control of their day-to-day work. It lays a heavy burden of responsibility on all concerned, but the success or failure of the

whole development of the island as a Reserve depends on it.

At the celebrations of his 90th birthday in July 1994, Max Nicholson, Director-General of the Nature Conservancy from 1952-66, looked back on the purchase of Rum and the environmental thinking which inspired the acquisition:

> As we struggled in the 1950s to teach ourselves what nature and nature conservation were, three things struck us forcibly: far less of 'wild nature' survived anywhere in Britain than we had vaguely supposed; of that remnant, human visitation, sport and even the lightest use were fast ending any dominance (or even surviving functioning) of truly natural ecological systems; and our practical, comprehensive knowledge of how ecology works – of population equilibrium, response to environmental change and interactions of competing species or of predators and prey – was practically nil. We were making it all up.

> The message was plain. If we were serious we must have a larger tract of totally separate land, on which visiting and living would be strictly controlled so as to minimise every kind of human impact not essential to research and conservation. Then we must carefully resuscitate habitats and entire communities, and let them show us how they chose to function. And we must, by a blend of toughness and persuasion, show all concerned that this was how it must be.

> Monica, Lady Bullough, had provided almost the only site in Britain where such conditions could possibly be approached. We grasped the opportunity and time has not yet shown that we failed in its pursuit.

CHAPTER 8

Regeneration of the Woodlands

IN APRIL 1997, exactly 40 years after the establishment of the island of Rum as a National Nature Reserve, a small event of large significance took place on the island: the ceremonial planting of a symbolic 'millionth tree' to commemorate 40 years of work to restore the biological productivity and diversity of the island through restoration of its woodlands.

It was the first formal event in the 40-year story of the NNR. Fittingly, the planting was done by Peter Wormell, the first Warden/ Naturalist on Rum (1957-73), with his wife Jessie, who had been the postmistress on the island when he arrived. Peter was responsible for starting the great woodland regeneration scheme which has profoundly altered the east side of the island around Loch Scresort and in Kinloch Glen.

The re-creation of a habitat resembling that which existed on Rum before the island was rendered treeless, largely by human activity, was and still is one of the main objectives of the management scheme for the National Nature Reserve. But it is not a question of planting just *any* trees holus-bolus all over the place and hoping that they will take root; they have to be trees which were once native to Rum.

So one of the earliest tasks was to build up a reliable picture of the island's vegetation in the past, through the study of pollen and plant remains which had survived in bogs.

This analysis showed that woodland developed on Rum soon after the end of the last Ice Age, 10,000 years ago. The picture which has emerged is of an island, 40% of whose surface was well forested on the north and east sides, and in Glen Harris to the west: a primeval mixed woodland of alder, ash, birch, hazel, juniper, oak, rowan, willow and wych elm occupying the sheltered glens and slopes, while the open ranges held bog myrtle, club mosses, grasses, sedges and, as the climate improved, an increasing number of flowering plants.

Woodland clearance probably began with the first farmers in Neolithic times. With the start of the Iron Age (around 400 BC in the Hebrides), metal tools became available to facilitate the task of felling and burning the forest to make room for pasturing livestock, and to provide fuel and building material. At the same time, from about 2000 BC onwards, the climate became cooler and wetter, which favoured the extension of poor quality wet heathland and would

Planting the 'millionth tree' on Rum:
Peter Wormell, with Magnus Magnusson

probably have caused a decrease in oak and wych elm without any human intervention.

Timothy Pont's 17th century sketch evidently showed four small woodlands and described the island as '*Montibus arduis et silvosis assurgens Ruma*' – 'Rum, rising up with its steep and wooded mountains'. In the *Old Statistical Account of Scotland* of 1796 a traditional Gaelic appellation for the island was recalled – 'Riogach na Forraiste an fiadhach', the 'Kingdom of the Wild Forest', where the Latin-derived term 'Forraiste' [*foresta*] probably refers to a hunting reserve rather than a wood; and the final destruction of the last copse was recorded (see CHAPTER 3). The combination of climate change and the removal by humans of the woodland cover resulted in a reduction in the diversity of flora and fauna in the trees and on the woodland floor; its contribution to the annual nutrient cycle probably dwindled, and soil quality progressively deteriorated.

By the time of the Rum Clearances (1826-28) there were only a few relict trees surviving: aspen, birch, hawthorn, holly, oak, rowan and willow, grimly hanging on to steep cliff-faces and rocky ravines where they were inaccessible to grazing and browsing and protected from fires.

When the island became a vast sheep-walk the pressure of intensive grazing hastened the severe impoverishment of the vegetation, apart from in gullies and inaccessible ravines. When sport took over as the main land-use on the island, with repeated heather-burning in an attempt to improve the habitat for deer and grouse, the destruction of the original vegetation cover was taken a stage further. Rum was now the epitome of Frank Fraser Darling's 'wet desert', described so depressingly in his *West Highland Survey*.

It was not until the 1850s that any attempt was made to reverse the process (even if only on a tiny scale), when Dr Lachlan Maclean planted an acre of sycamores, beeches, ash and elms around the former Kinloch house; 50 years later this copse had come to be known as 'The Park'. Over the years these trees have grown into magnificent specimens which stand proudly behind the present Post Office. In the 1890s John Bullough and his son, Sir George Bullough, guided by the naturalist J A Harvie-Brown, planted a large area on the north and south shores of

Loch Scresort to provide a bosky setting for Kinloch Castle – 120 species in all, a total of 80,000 mixed conifers and deciduous trees.

Not all of them survived; but of the 120 species planted, 50 have regenerated naturally. Many of the trees have grown to noble proportions, and the old woodland now throbs with birdlife: not just the 'common-or-garden' blackbirds, blue tits, chaffinches, robins and song thrushes, but chiffchaffs, goldcrests, spotted flycatchers, treecreepers, willow warblers and wood warblers with their silvery jingle.

Goldcrest

The planting of these policy woodlands to improve the environs of Kinloch Castle was the start, unwittingly perhaps, of the restoration of the biodiversity of the island.

The restoration programme

One of the Nature Conservancy's priorities when it acquired the island in 1957 was the large-scale woodland restoration programme aimed at re-creating forest formations composed of native trees and shrubs in appropriate parts of the island.

Because native trees and shrubs of local origin were unobtainable commercially, Peter Wormell began by establishing a tree nursery for native species. It meant developing new techniques of raising native trees of local provenance for specific use in creating a new native woodland habitats. In three long seed-beds he sowed pine seeds (from Loch Maree), and birch and alder seeds from Rum. Soon the nursery was producing 50,000 seedlings a year, of twenty species, each one requiring individual treatment for successful germination and growth. It meant having to create new techniques for the propagation of native trees from seed; these techniques were subsequently taken up and developed by other nurseries. All the seeds are now hand-collected on the island.

Before the nursery was in full production, however, the first transplantings took place, in April 1958. At the head of Kilmory Glen, Peter dug the holes for his wife Jessie to plant 100 seedling birches which were growing naturally in the woods behind Kinloch Castle. It was a practical earnest of the future. They all survived and are now 50 feet high!

Peter then created a series of trial planting plots: three at Kilmory, one at Harris and one at Kinloch, followed by two tiny plots high on Ard Nev and Ard-mheall. It was quickly apparent that the trial plots were succeeding, and the decision was made to fence off some 640 hectares of Mullach Mòr, the headland to the north of Kinloch, to protect it from browsing by deer. It was a very boggy area, with remnants of the native woodland surviving only on crags, and an area from which it was very difficult to extract venison.

The site had to be prepared by hand, to start with, by turning over the turf; later, ploughing was undertaken, in patches, to break the surface. The planting programme included mainly Scots pine, birch, alder and oak, with ash, aspen, bird cherry, elm, gean, grey sallow and other willows, guelder rose, hawthorn, hazel, holly, juniper and sloe as associates. It involved planting 60,000 trees a year eventually, in harsh winter conditions; the work was undertaken by three or four estate workers on top of their regular work on the estate.

The planting programme in the exclosure to the north of Kinloch was dealt a terrible blow by a huge fire which swept through north-east Rum in March 1969. Peter and his staff had been doing routine burning of the fire-breaks when the wind changed and they lost control. Nearly 200,000 trees – some seven years of planting – went up in flames. Astonishingly, although much of the conifer wood was destroyed, the deciduous trees survived; they were coaxed back to life by coppicing, and the programme was completed by 1977. A second exclosure was created by Peter's successors to the south of Kinloch, between Loch Scresort and Welshman's Rock, encompassing another 400 hectares. Planting will be completed by the end of the century.[1]

Scots pine seedling

More than a million trees have now been planted. The oak-tree planted by Peter Wormell on a hillside overlooking Kinloch Castle in April 1997 was a symbol of the island's revived capacity to cope with the more demanding tree species where the ground has been improved by the planting of pioneer species such as birch, alder and willow. Some of the planting has been helped by the use of 'nurse species' like lodgepole pine, which created a woodland environment and assisted the more sensitive native species to thrive; these 'nurse species' are being removed when their task has been completed.

Already a real woodland flora is flourishing under the trees where once there was only heather and moor grass (see CHAPTER 9). The trees have also created a new habitat for the insects which thrive in the nooks and crannies of the forest (see CHAPTER 13), and for the woodland birds which had disappeared completely from the island (see CHAPTER 10).

The re-creation of the forest habitats of Rum is well on its way, but it is not going to be easy. A major constraint is the current level of grazing. Red deer, feral goats and Highland cattle are all present; some of them, particularly the cattle, play an important role in the maintenance of natural diversity. However, the populations of red deer can hinder

[1] *Peter Wormell left Rum in 1973 to become NCC Assistant Regional Officer for Argyll. He retired from the NCC in 1990.*

the recovery of the vegetation communities. Scottish Natural Heritage is committed to a substantial reduction in the numbers of red deer on Rum, to allow the trees and their associated ground flora to regenerate naturally.

It is all an integral part of the vision of full island regeneration which Scottish Natural Heritage is determined to bring to fruition over the decades to come (see CHAPTER 16).

CHAPTER 9

Rum in Flower

FOR THE NATURALIST, a truly charming aspect of Rum is the tremendous range of conditions supporting a most varied flora within a comparatively small compass: a highly varied geology and soil base exposed in precipitous sea-cliffs and rugged peaks, deep sheltered glens and sandy bays, hill lochans and burns, and a geographical position in the path of oceanic weather systems and mild Atlantic Drift waters. There is no other island of comparable size around our shores with such an exciting combination and complexity of geology, landform, altitude, climate, soil and land-use history. On Rum the botany ranges from both relic and restored woodland flora, through the plants of the grasslands, heaths and marshes, and up to the arctic montane flora, all with their own specialities and special pleasures. [1]

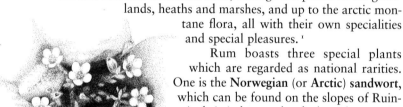

Norwegian (or Arctic) sandwort

Rum boasts three special plants which are regarded as national rarities. One is the **Norwegian** (or **Arctic**) **sandwort**, which can be found on the slopes of Ruinsival; it is low and tufted, with opposite pairs of rather fleshy, oblong leaves and shining white, five-petalled flowers. The second is the **Lapland marsh orchid**, a beautiful little plant first recognised in Scotland in 1988; it looks not unlike the northern marsh orchid but with a more stunted head of magenta-to-purple flowers with crimson lines, rings and splotches, and purple-blotched leaves.

The third is an **eyebright**, *Euphrasia heslop-harrisonii*, a bonny little plant with white flowers suffused with purple and yellow; it is a micro-species of very specialist interest – and many specialists would confess that they wouldn't recognise it if they saw it. It grows at only one known spot on Rum, on the shores of Loch Scresort where the rushes meet the sea.

But for the amateur botanist the delights lie not in rooting around for rarities but coming across such a rich variety of plants, however familiar, in this unique island setting.

[1] *In terms of numbers, more than 2,200 species of plants (including lichens and fungi) have been recorded – and the list grows year by year.*

Flora of the woodlands

In the predominantly treeless landscape of Rum there are some surprising and delightful pockets of woodland flowers which visitors will meet just a short walk from the landing stage. The 'last copse on Rum' had been cleared by 1796, and the island was virtually devoid of trees for about 50 years until, in the 1850s, new owners planted an acre of the large sycamores, beeches and elms which stand today behind the Post Office on the site of the old Kinloch House (see CHAPTER 3). A century and a half later, this inspired plantation provides a spring carpet of woodland bluebells in 'treeless' Rum.

But small fragments of natural scrub of birch, rowan, hazel, holly, oak and willow had survived in steep gullies and cliff ledges where they were inaccessible to grazing animals and protected from fires. In the glens of Shellesder, Kinloch, Kilmory, Camas Pliasgaig and Caves Bay there was significant survival of a woodland field layer: angelica, bluebell, common dog violet, primrose, stitchwort, wood-sorrel, and yellow pimpernel.

Several other woodland plants managed to survive in shady places along the coast even where no trees remained, such as slender false brome, hay scented buckler-fern, bugle (which was once regarded as a sovereign cure for hangovers!), red campion, lesser celandine, dog's mercury, wild garlic, valerian (which has been used since Roman times to treat stress) and water avens.

In the early years of this century the Bullough family greatly expanded the policy plantations around Kinloch Castle and the head of Loch Scresort – predominantly Scots and Corsican pines, larch, lime, Norway maple, Norway spruce, sycamore, horse chestnut and even sweet chestnut. These policy woodlands did not resemble the traditional natural forest which had disappeared but they enabled many of the native woodland plants to survive. A whole woodland flora began to make its presence felt under the young trees; other local woodland plants, like wood anemone and wood-sedge, are rarely found outside the Kinloch woods. This pioneer bridgehead for woodland flora is now being powerfully reinforced by the woodland regeneration schemes of 40 years' standing (see CHAPTER 8).

Maritime grasslands, heaths and marshes

A walk in any direction from Kinloch brings you to open country. To the north, Kilmory Glen leads down to a sandy strand and maritime grasslands. This is one of the botanical 'hot-spots' on Rum – the machair, a grassy plain rich in wild carrot, field gentian and kidney vetch. The heath knolls have wild thyme, bird's-foot-trefoil and the charmingly-named self heal with its reddish-purple 'throat'-shaped flowers, which was used in medieval Europe to staunch bleeding and as a gargle for sore throats. This is the best area in which to see the greatest variety of plants of maritime grasslands, heaths and marshes, including (locally) the splendid Grass of Parnassus.

To the west of Kilmory Glen is Sgaorishal and Monadh Dubh – another 'hot-spot'. As in the north-east, wet heath and blanket bog predominate, with fine stands of bog asphodel; but there is also a limestone ridge running down to the west coast where the beautiful white-petalled mountain avens grows on steep lime-rich sea-cliffs and grassy banks.

Gullies in the sea-cliffs provide the main habitat for the scaly male-fern, lady-fern, mountain male-fern and royal fern – a group of plants which dominated the landscape of Scotland when dinosaurs, rather than deer, grazed the land. Another fern, forked spleenwort, was discovered on Rum only within the past 25 years (it was almost certainly overlooked because it grows inconspicuously in crevices in the hard igneous rocks). It has disappeared from some of its other Scottish sites because of shade created by tree-planting and the spread of shrub, but it still exists abundantly on the warm, south-west facing rocks of Holyrood Park in the heart of Edinburgh.

The wood bitter-vetch is also found on sea-cliff ledges on Rum. This sprawling plant has white flowers with purple veins and is usually found

Wood sorrel

in meadows or scrub. Now uncommon in Britain and rapidly declining, it is one of several 'Atlantic' species with a stronghold in the west of Scotland. Rum also has an important range of mosses and ferns, like the hay-scented buckler and the tiny Tunbridge filmy fern.

Another scarce and attractive plant of the sea-cliff terraces is the pyramidal bugle, which is small and hairy with a striking head of lilac-blue flowers. Within Britain it is rarely found outside the north-west of Scotland.

The grasslands and herb-rich heaths of Glen Harris have a variety of meadow grasses including crested hair-grass and heath-grass; in summer they are ablaze with common flowers such as eyebrights, milkwort, purple thyme, yellow trefoils, vetches – and orchids, among them the white lesser butterfly orchid and the purple fragrant orchid. Harebells can be found in small numbers, but only at the Bullough Mausoleum plot at Harris during July.

Alpine flora

The mountain flowers provide the most distinctive element of the flora of Rum – the fewest in number but the most special botanically; but they are much harder to reach than other plants.

A favoured area for montane flowers must be the south-west with its towering peaks – Orval, Ard Nev and Sròn an t-Saighdeir to the north of Harris, and Ainshval, Sgùrr nan Gillean and Ruinsival to the south. All these summits have patches of well-grazed and wind-pruned tundra-like vegetation. Among the mat-grass are bilberry and crowberry in the drier areas, and rushes, mountain sedges and dwarf willow in the wetter parts. On the summits of Ard Nev and Orval there is a well-developed 'fjellfield' with fine carpets of Alpine clubmoss.

Perhaps the most accessible area for non-mountaineers is the north-east cliff of Fionchra, overlooking Glen Shellesder, where in summer you can find rich displays of the leggy, white-flowered mossy saxifrage, named after its moss-like leaves. On bluffs of harder rock nearby there are a few plants of the altogether stiffer and less showy alpine saxifrage. In early spring the cliffs come to life with vivid patches of purple saxifrage (the most attractive of the mountain saxifrages with its rosy-purple flowers), and the odd flower may last into early summer among its creeping, mossy stems. You also find speedwell with its tiny, rich blue flowers, and alpine meadow-rue, which prefers damper areas.

One of the more noteworthy plants there is alpine penny-cress, which is largely restricted to the northern Pennines and Lake District and is known on only three sites in Scotland; recognisable from its glossy spoon-shaped leaves held in an untidy rosette on the ground, on Rum it grows on one small area of calcareous rock on Fionchra. The cliff ledges also have tall herbs more commonly associated with woodland, such as meadowsweet with its creamy-white flowers; and because it is relatively low and near the sea, there are roseroot with its greenish-yellow flowers and the ubiquitous sea-pink (thrift).

Purple saxifrage

Two other plants stand out: Scottish asphodel and mossy cyphel. **Scottish asphodel** is not quite exclusively Scottish, despite its name; it is a delicate little perennial, with a very tight head of greenish-white flowers. It is a very localised plant of lime-rich mountain springs and flushes at altitudes of 200-900m. **Mossy cyphel** is a neat cushion plant which looks remarkably moss-like when not in flower; in blossom, however, the cushions are adorned with a mass of creamy star-shaped flowers. It is common in open gravel soils in Scottish mountains as well as in the Alps and the Pyrenees.

High up on the slopes of Hallival and Askival and the towering summit of Trollaval, Rum's teeming colonies of Manx shearwaters breed in a tumult of nesting burrows (see CHAPTER 10). Over the centuries the birds' droppings have manured the soil and produced areas of vivid emerald-green grassland which provide rich high-altitude pastures. These 'shearwater greens' are well-grazed by deer but still support herbs and grasses more characteristic of lowland grasslands, with species like heath bedstraw, dog violet and heath speedwell.

In contrast, on the unstable rocky surfaces beyond the 'shearwater greens' the vegetation is much sparser. Here can be found another rare plant, northern rock-cress, a member of the cabbage family, which is as common on Rum as it is scarce elsewhere – a burst of white four-petalled flowers coming to life in lush patches on gravelly windswept mountain shoulders. Another characteristic flower of the west is mountain ever-lasting, which grows almost from sea-level to the tops of the hills. Among the purple moor-grass and heath-grass starred with yellow tor-mentil and wild thyme one can find other alpine plants which thrive on these soils: alpine ladies-mantle, stone bramble and mountain sorrel, as well as showy tufts of moss campion with shiny green leaves and mass-es of rosy-red flowers in early summer.

The sandstone hills of Mullach Ard and Mullach Mòr in northern and eastern Rum have peaty soils which support wet heath and blanket bog with flushes of purple moor-grass. The bogs are rich in sphagnum mosses and sedges, as well as insectivorous sundews and pink butter-wort. The wet heaths support an impressive display of deep yellow bog asphodel and pale lilac heath spotted orchids among blue milkwort, yellow tormentil, and purple bell heather and cross-leaved heath. The deep-er peats are more interesting botanically, having escaped the ravages of fire and heavy grazing, and some still support the fragile hummock-forming sphagnum mosses, cottongrasses and many bog sedges, includ-ing white beak-sedge and, in one location, the rare brown beak-sedge.

Pillwort

The summer of 1997 saw the return of an aquatic speciality previously lost from the botanical checklist of 630 flowering plants, ferns and stoneworts: pillwort, *Pilularia globulifera*. This small, primitive fresh-water fern, which grows mainly in lowland lochs and ponds, gets its name from the small reproductive 'pills' produced in late summer at the base of the thread-like green fronds. Although individual plants are inconspicuous, pillwort can grow in abundance in favourable condi-tions, forming bright green 'lawns' on mud or silt at loch margins.

Pillwort is one of the species selected by Scottish Natural Heritage for special treatment in its Species Action Programme, which provides a co-ordinated approach to the conservation of Scotland's most threat-ened wildlife and aims to maintain or restore viable populations of pri-ority species across their traditional range. It inhabits the shallow, muddy margins of lochs and ponds, but has been declining since the

1970s and is now scarce in Britain.

Pillwort was previously recorded at several lochans on Rum, but probably disappeared when cattle were removed from the island. The cattle ponds in Glen Harris are among the lost sites, and the reintroduction of Highland cattle to the island in 1971 (see CHAPTER 12) has restored them to ideal habitats for pillwort. The cattle trample ('poach') the margins of the ponds as they come to drink, and so maintain the open mud in which pillwort can flourish.

The reintroduction was effected in co-operation with Plantlife, the wild-plant conservation charity, and the plants were restored to their habitat by Sue Scott, the marine biologist and wife of the Scottish Officer of Plantlife, botanist and writer Michael Scott. This tiny fern may not be one of the most showy members of Rum's rich flora, but its return marks another significant step in the long-term restoration of the biodiversity of Rum.

CHAPTER 10

Birdlife

RUM OFFERS A FASCINATING VARIETY of habitats for birds. The total number of species recorded from, or adjacent to, the island currently stands at 202; up to 95 of these have bred on Rum at one time or another, and 63 breed regularly. About half of the regular breeders are small song birds in the woodland around Kinloch; many of the others are waders and seabirds. Another 18 species breed on Rum sporadically.

Two bird species in particular claim special interest: Manx shearwaters, and white-tailed (or sea) eagles.

Shearwaters: the Manxies of the mountains

The upper slopes of the mountains in the southern half of the island are the summer home of one of the largest breeding colonies in Britain of a remarkable oceanic seabird, the Manx shearwater. Not only that: it holds about 20 per cent of the world's population of these shearwaters. Not many National Nature Reserves in Britain can boast a fifth of the world population of a particular species!

The Rum colony is unique in Britain because the birds nest at altitudes of between 350 and 800 metres, and up to three kilometres from the sea. The conical peaks of Hallival and Askival with their connecting ridge and the towering summit of Trollaval (especially the north and east facing slopes) support the great majority of the birds; there are also nesting burrows on Barkeval, Bloodstone Hill, Fionchra and Ruinsival. The ground is rugged and steep, comprising rocky outcrops, crags, boulder fields, bare eroded slopes, scree fields and terraces; the basic igneous rocks have been decomposed by the windy, humid climate into a rich brown sand and gravelly soil, and it is in this soil that the shearwaters excavate their nesting burrows.

Manx shearwater

What an unlikely habitat in which to make a home! And what remarkable creatures they are. Every year they travel half-way round the world to winter on the South Atlantic waters off southern Brazil and Argentina. They cover immense distances in a seemingly effortless gliding flight, skimming so low over the waves that the tips of their long narrow wings 'shear the water'. Shearwaters are long-lived and generally pair for life, most of them returning to the same nest-burrow year after year; every spring more than 60,000 pairs return to nest on Rum. In the long summer evenings huge concentrations of the birds assemble on the sea in rafts, thousands strong, between Rum and Eigg, awaiting nightfall before returning to their burrows inland; as night falls they fly in to incubate their single white egg and, later, to feed their solitary chick.

Shearwaters are usually silent while at sea. But at night, high up in the mountains, they set up the most extraordinary noise imaginable: an unearthly chorus of cackling and shrieking as they fly in to be greeted by their mates or youngsters underground. It has been suggested that the Norse name for the central Cuillin – Trollaval ('Trolls' Mountain') – was inspired by superstitious awe of the eerie pandemonium of the shearwaters in their subterranean nesting-holes. Certainly, three place-names in the Faroes which incorporate the prefix 'Troll-' are also associated with shearwater colonies.

For those who encounter the shearwaters on Rum at night the experience is unforgettable. One of SNH's senior ecologists, Des Thompson, first met the Manxies when he was a 15-year-old schoolboy camping on Rum with the Schools' Hebridean Society. Along with two others he spent a couple of August nights in a tiny wooden bothy high up on Hallival. They left the bothy at about 11 pm in ferocious weather and darkness, and clambered towards the summit; all around them they could hear the most alarming growls and caterwaulings from the ground under their feet and in the air around them. As banks of clouds scudded past the hill, scores of birds fled down into their burrows, so oblivious of the boys that some crashed into them – anything to get to their burrows. The adults were flying in and responding to the youngsters in the burrows, or those adults which had been incubating the eggs (for days, sometimes) were trying to guide their mates back to the right burrow to take over (the males are particularly vocal!). It is a miracle of night-flying and precise navigation. When the boys returned to the bothy, soaked and exhilarated, they were kept awake for the rest of the night – by three young shearwaters in nests which had been made right under the floorboards of the bothy!

As it nears fledging, the single chick grows big and fat. It is occasionally fed on regurgitated semi-digested fish and squid brought in by one or other of its parents. Some youngsters become so obese that the exit hole is too small for their departure. At that stage the parents abandon their offspring, or feed it less frequently. Only when it has used up some surplus fat does the chick emerge on to the dark hillside to exercise its wings. After a couple of weeks it starts looking for a suitable runway, making its ungainly way upwards among the rocks and boulders, waiting for an encouraging breeze. Eventually it clambers on top of a boulder and launches itself down the mountain towards the sea. It is a long and hazardous journey across inhospitable moorland, and the casualty rate can be high.

Shearwaters are seabirds *par excellence*; they never go ashore except to breed or as storm-blown vagrants after heavy gales. Fast and agile on the wing, they can easily commute 360 km each way from the colony on a day's feeding trip. By contrast they are remarkably awkward on land, propelling themselves with their feet in an ungainly shuffle on their wings and belly; this makes them extremely vulnerable on the ground. Their main predators are golden eagles, great black-backed gulls and peregrines – and, surprisingly, red deer; the deer will sometimes kill chicks when they emerge from their burrows and eat the heads and legs for calcium, leaving the rest of the carcasses for eagles, ravens and hooded crows to pick up at dawn.

There are good pickings all round at the shearwater colony. The birds' nutrient-rich droppings, deposited over many centuries, have fertilised the soil and produced areas of vivid emerald-green grassland which provide rich high-altitude pastures. These 'shearwater greens', as they are called, support invertebrates, birds and mammals which would otherwise not survive at these altitudes: red deer crop the vegetation down to a short springy turf, pygmy shrews feed on insects and other invertebrates, brown rats move up in autumn to scavenge on the debris of the nesting season, and migrant song thrushes have been seen hopping over the greens as though they were feeding on a garden lawn. Meadow pipits often flock there and wheatears benefit from the abundance of invertebrates, while wrens breed among the boulder fields adjoining the shearwater colonies.

Just by being there, the shearwaters have created their own distinctive and unlikely habitat on the mountain tops of Rum. It is a strange feeling, to be treading warily over boulders and shattered rocks, knowing that shearwaters are lying low under your feet, keeping quiet until the evening performance.

White-tailed (sea) eagles

Rum was the location for the reintroduction the largest bird of prey in Britain: the sea eagle, or white-tailed eagle, with its brilliant white tail, its yellow feet and beak and its piercing yellow gaze. In Gaelic it is known as *iolaire sùil na grèine* – 'the eagle with the sunlit eye': a wonderfully evocative name for a magnificent creature.

The sea eagle is the fourth largest eagle in the world; its wingspan is nearly two and a half metres, whereas that of the golden eagle rarely exceeds two metres. It is an awe-inspiring bird capable of striking acrobatic behaviour. Its aerial courtship in early spring involves spectacular feats of talon-gripping and cartwheeling, accompanied by much excited yelping.

The sea eagle was once a familiar sight over much of Scotland. Increasing human pressure, and the subsequent loss of habitat through changes in farming systems, changed all that; by the beginning of the 19th century populations of sea eagles were to be found only along the north and west coasts of Scotland and Ireland. Isolated pairs elsewhere were subjected to ruthless persecution, through shooting, poisoning and trapping. In places where the eyries were reasonably accessible, like Galloway and Orkney, the birds were driven rapidly towards extinction by the spread of sheep-farming and at the hands of land managers generally, determined to exter-

White-tailed (sea) eagle

minate all predators regardless of whether or not there was any evidence that they affected commercially valuable creatures. Victorian naturalists hastened the process by their eagerness to collect the eggs and have the skins of this increasingly rare species stuffed as trophies.

On Rum the sea eagle fared no better than anywhere else. It is recorded that, in the late 1820s, one of the Rum shepherds shot five birds in one day, while in 1866 a local gamekeeper shot eight. When John Bullough bought Rum in 1888 his staff were encouraged to adopt a more tolerant attitude towards predators; his son, Sir George Bullough, reverted to the more traditional approach and in 1907 his keeper shot an adult sea eagle and collected two eggs from its cliff eyrie. The female found a new mate, but both eagles were shot two years later on the island's west coast.

By the early 1900s only a few isolated breeding sea eagles remained. The last known breeding attempt by native birds was made on the neighbouring island of Skye in 1916. Two years later the last surviving British sea eagle, an ageing albino female, was shot at her lonely eyrie in Shetland.

After the Second World War the re-establishment of a sea eagle population in Britain came to be considered a nature conservation priority. It was considered unlikely that it would ever recolonise Scotland naturally, unlike the migratory osprey which returned to Scotland in the 1950s. So in 1959 the first, small-scale attempt at reintroduction was made, when three birds were released at Loch Etive, Argyll; two of them died, while the third, the only adult, was recaptured and taken to a zoo. In 1968 the naturalist George Waterston released four young Norwegian birds on Fair Isle, but none survived. The failure of both attempts at reintroduction is thought to have been because too few birds were released, and because the programmes were not carried forward.

Valuable lessons had been learned, however, and by 1973 a third attempt was being planned, because it was believed that post-war protection measures for wild birds, as well as changes in land use and human attitudes in western Scotland, would have reduced the risk of the kind of persecution which had driven the bird to extinction. Furthermore, the availability of nest sites and the food supply were believed to be at least as high as in the 19th century.

In 1975 the Nature Conservancy Council (NCC) instigated a major reintroduction programme, using the island of Rum as the release location; the project officer in charge was John Love.

The northern stronghold of the sea eagle is Norway, with more than 1,500 pairs, and the Norwegian Directorate for Nature Management, with great generosity, granted licences for eaglets to be collected there by Harald Misund, a Norwegian naturalist, in co-operation with SNH's John Love. In the first year four 8-week-old eaglets were flown from Bodø, in north Norway, to Scotland by 120 Squadron of RAF Kinloss and taken to Rum for rearing and release. The birds were housed during their five-week statutory quarantine period in specially constructed cages, in which they were fed on a natural diet of fish, supplemented with rabbit and venison. Throughout their captivity (during which the only male bird died, alas) great care was taken to avoid human contact, to minimise the risk that the birds might 'imprint' on their human helpers. The three surviving eaglets were released in the autumn from a rock beside the road above Loch an Dornabac: one was subsequently found dead under an overhead power cable in Morven, but the other two adapted well to life in the wild.

In the following year another ten eaglets were received from Norway and released. The Rum project continued from 1975 to 1985, during which time 82 birds, all from Norway, were released; three had died in captivity. Seven birds are known to have died shortly after release, two of them through poisoning. Some released juveniles wandered widely, but at three to four years old the birds settled on fixed home ranges within 100 km of the release site on Rum.

Sea eagles take about five years to mature, so it was several years before the youngsters released on Rum began to form breeding pairs. The first eggs were laid in 1983, but failed to hatch, as did two clutches in 1984. However, in 1985 a pair of the birds released from Rum successfully reared a single chick, the first to be fledged in the wild in Scotland for about 70 years.

After careful evaluation of the first phase of the project (1975-85) the reintroduction programme was resumed in 1993, but not on Rum; a new release site was selected in a secluded locality in the north-west. Ten young birds were released, and the programme is still continuing;

by 1997, 47 birds from the second release site had taken wing to search out their own territories across Scotland.

Since the first success in 1985 a total of 66 chicks have been fledged in Scotland. For security reasons the locations of the nesting sites are not revealed; but they have spread far and wide over the Western Isles and the west coast of Scotland. In 1996 a juvenile sea eagle flew over Glasgow city centre, another paid a visit to a bald eagle at the Bird of Prey Centre near Beauly, and a third was seen attacking a fox near Dingwall. In 1996, in fact, there were twelve pairs (or trios – some of the males are bigamous) of territory-holding sea eagles, of which seven were successful in rearing nine chicks. In addition, young birds raised in the wild in Scotland are now starting to enter the breeding population. A few of the Scottish-released birds have, as expected, made their way back to Norway.

The reintroduction of the sea eagle has been one of the spectacular success stories of nature conservation this century. The resident breeding population is still small and still very vulnerable: one of the reintroduced birds was found poisoned in July, 1996, and egg-collectors have been causing problems for some pairs. Despite these setbacks the population continues to strengthen, albeit very slowly, and there is every hope that in time it will be securely re-established throughout much of its former range as a viable and visible part of Scotland's natural heritage.

And that is as it should be. From earliest times the sea eagle has been a potent symbol in Scotland. In prehistoric Orkney it was given totem status: in a Bronze Age chambered tomb at Isbister on South Ronaldsay, known as 'the Tomb of the Eagles', remains of sea eagles were interred with human remains, and sea eagles were later depicted on several Pictish stone carvings. So sea eagles had a long and cherished place in human culture before being driven from our shores – and Scottish Natural Heritage is now striving, with others, to restore them to their proper place.

Moorland birds

Like the sea eagle, golden eagles were persecuted on Rum while it was managed as a sporting estate, but as that era drew to a close they reappeared in their former territories. All the eyries found on Rum today are on cliff ledges, and two pairs breed regularly (and usually successfully), although four pairs have occasionally bred.

There are comparatively few birds of prey on Rum, due to the scarcity of small mammal species. There are two or three pairs of merlins, kestrels and peregrines which breed regularly, and long-eared and short-eared owls nest intermittently.

The raven, that enigmatic baron of the uplands, is a lordly resident of both the hinterland and coastal areas, congregating in grave assemblies in the autumn.

The characteristic breeding birds of the moors are golden plovers, meadow pipits and snipe, while the numbers of nesting curlews are gradually increasing. Stonechat and wheatear, meadow pipit and rock pipit, twite and skylark, occur in the glens and coastal areas; along the burns and lochs one can see dipper and common sandpiper, with ring ouzel on the higher ground. The cuckoo is a regular arrival at the end of April and the males sing without cease well into June, while the females lay their eggs (usually) in meadow pipits' nests. Winter brings the delightful snow bunting, fluttering about like a snowflake in the wind.

Red-throated diver

The lochs now attract an encouraging number of red-throated divers. The red-throated diver with its weird, wailing call suffered from persecution on the island, but the establishment of the National Nature Reserve allowed them to reappear in numbers, and now some ten pairs breed regularly. It is still a fragile population, and crows are quick to snatch unattended eggs if the adult is disturbed by anglers or walkers, so access to some of the lochs is restricted as soon as it is known that divers are breeding there. In the same way, tree-planting is carefully restricted in order to keep the banks of the lochs clear.

Red grouse were plentiful while Rum was a sporting estate, when captive-reared birds were regularly released for the benefit of the guns. Because of the poor heather cover, Rum supports fewer than a hundred pairs. Snipe and woodcock are relatively common, and now that the woodlands are maturing it should not be long before more male woodcocks will be seen 'roding' (performing their breeding display flights) at dusk.

Seabirds

Apart from its Manx shearwaters, Rum has a rich assemblage of breeding seabirds, with a total breeding population of about 130,000 individuals of 12 seabird species. The sea-cliffs are tenement homes to guillemots, razorbills, fulmars (in ever-increasing numbers) and dense colonies of kittiwakes chattering like children in a school playground. Shags nest in scattered colonies among coastal boulderfields all around the island. There are also small numbers of puffins, and both common and arctic terns are occasional breeders. A few cormorants and gannets may be seen offshore.

Gulls are ubiquitous, mainly herring gulls and lesser blackbacks. The misnamed common gull is not very common, and some great black-backed gulls occur.

Woodland birds

The establishment of the Kinloch policy woodlands a hundred years ago enabled many woodland birds to colonise the island, and many of these species have now moved into the planted woodland around Kinloch. The commonest birds seem to be blackbirds, chaffinches, dunnocks, goldcrests, robins, willow warblers and wrens. Blackcaps, blue tits, coal tits, mistle thrushes, song thrushes, spotted flycatchers and treecreepers are becoming increasingly common in the more mature parts of the north side plantings and in the experimental plots, and one can also see bullfinches, chiffchaffs, garden warblers, grasshopper warblers, greenfinches, reed buntings, siskins, whinchats, whitethroats and wood warblers.

None of the more distant Hebridean islands has large, mature woodlands, so who knows what other species will settle on Rum in the future and breed?

Birds of the shore

On the shore one can see bar-tailed godwit, common sandpiper, curlew, dunlin, grey plover, heron (which nest in the trees around Kinloch), oystercatcher, redshank, ringed plover, rock dove, sanderling, shelduck and whimbrel. Hooded crows abound all over the island, nesting on crags or in trees. Out at sea, in the sheltered waters of Loch Scresort, eider ducks dive to feed, the drakes black and white and the ducks brown; several pairs nest above the shore and on the hill-slopes at the mouth of Loch Scresort, and some even nest in the ruined cottages of Port nan Carannan. Red-breasted mergansers are also to be seen, sometimes in small flocks beating their wings to 'herd' shoals of small fish; some of them nest in the woodlands on the southern shore of Loch Scresort.

Eider duck (male)

CHAPTER 11

Red Deer on Rum

FOR MANY PEOPLE Rum and red deer are inseparably linked – and rightly so: the intensive study of the island's red deer represents one of the longest-running and most significant studies of a large mammal anywhere in the world. Over the years, the deer research on Rum has consistently been at the forefront of research on mammal ecology. It has made a substantial contribution to our understanding of the interaction between animal populations and their environment, and has helped to lay the foundation for scientific management of animal populations, both in Britain and overseas.

There have been deer on Rum since time immemorial. Their bones are found in large numbers in the cave at Bàgh na h-Uamha (see CHAPTER 2). A detailed Description of the Hebrides commissioned by King James VI (c.1580) noted that Rum was 'an ile of small profit... the hills and waist glennis are commodious only for the hunting of deir'.

There is other evidence that the hunting of deer was a factor in island life in the 16th century. In 1549 a 'pious and well-informed' Dean of the Isles, Donald Monro, wrote about Rum in his 'Account of the Western Isles of Scotland', which was published in Martin Martin's *A Description of the Western Isles of Scotland called Hybrides* (1703). He found:

> a forest full of high mountains and abundance of little deers in it, which deers will never be slain downwith, but the principal settis [seats] must be in the height of the hills, because the deer will be called upwards always by the tinchel, or without the tinchel they will pass up.[1]

Dean Monro was describing stone-walled deer-traps he called 'settis', or seats. The hunting of deer was evidently done by a form of deer-driving (the 'tinchel') which was a popular and effective event in the Highlands of Scotland, serving not only as a source of venison but as a sport.

In 1796 the *Old Statistical Account of Scotland* described their mode of operation:

> Before the use of fire arms, their method of killing deer was as follows: On each side of a glen, formed by two mountains, stone dykes were begun pretty high in the mountains, and carried to the lower part of the valley, always drawing nearer, till within 3 or 4 feet of each other. From this narrow pass, a circular space was inclosed by a stone wall, of a height sufficient to confine the deer; to this place they were pur-

[1] *the spelling has been modernised*

sued and destroyed. The vestige of one of these inclosures is still to be seen in Rum.

Dean Monro may well have been referring to a structure which still survives on the south slopes of Orval, 400m above sea level. The heath on the summit offers attractive grazing for deer, and a narrow strip extends down the steep slope. Its edges have been built up with boulders from the loose scree on either side, and converge towards a complex drystane enclosure, nearly 12m in diameter, with high stone walls which, even in their present semi-ruinous state, reach a height of about 2m. There is what could be another deer-trap on the slopes of Orval and Ard Nev above Loch a' Ghille Reamhra. In 1995, Historic Scotland conducted a field survey which identified another two possible deer-traps, on Sgòrr Rèidh and Sròn an t-Saighdeir, which have now been scheduled as being of national importance.

By these 'tinchels' (or 'tainchels') and other methods, all the red deer on Rum had been exterminated by the 1780s. The English naturalist Thomas Pennant noted in 1771 that their numbers had been reduced to about 80 (*A tour in Scotland and voyage to the Hebrides*, 1772), and Edward Daniel Clarke, the Cambridge geologist, reported their eventual extinction some 15 years later (*Life and remains of Edward Daniel Clarke DD*, 1834). The *Old Statistical Account of Scotland* noted in 1796:

> In Rum there were formerly great numbers of deer; there was also a copse of wood, that afforded cover to their fawns from birds of prey, particularly from the eagle: While the wood throve, the deer also throve; now that the wood is totally destroyed, the deer are extirpated.

So by the end of the 18th century there were no deer on Rum. But Rum would remain without deer for only half a century. Nearly 20 years after Rum had been cleared of its indigenous population (see CHAPTER 3) and turned into a sheep-run, the Marquis of Salisbury bought the island in 1845 because he saw Rum's potential as a deer 'forest', and immediately set about transforming the island into a typical Victorian Highland estate with an emphasis on field sports. Salisbury successfully reintroduced red deer by importing them from mainland estates in Scotland, mainly from Ross-shire; he also imported deer from English parks, but they failed to rear their offspring in the harsher conditions of Rum. He tried to introduce fallow deer, too, but they failed to thrive.

Deer numbers rose as the island developed as a sporting estate and there were several further importations of stags from English deer parks as John Bullough, and subsequently his son George, continued to develop the island, right through to the late 1920s. Around 40 stags and 40 hinds were culled annually. Deer numbers were maintained at between 1,200 and 1,700. When Rum passed into public ownership in 1957 there were some 1,600 red deer on the island. There were also about 2,000 sheep.

Deer research on Rum

The red deer is Scotland's largest and most visible land mammal. Away back in the 1930s, Frank Fraser Darling was refused permission (by Sir George Bullough) to use Rum to carry out his pio-neering research on red deer; this resulted in him having to work on deer in Wester Ross for his classic study, *A Herd of Red Deer* (1937).

Red deer stag

When the Nature Conservancy acquired Rum, however, not a great deal was known about red deer or how they lived; Fraser Darling's work provided a lyri-cal synthesis of existing knowledge, but con-tained little quantitative information. At that stage there were no precise estimates of the age at which deer started breeding, of changes in breeding success with age or of their normal lifespan, partly because reliable techniques for determining the age of animals had not yet been developed. Their food plants had been listed – but no one had tried to measure the relative importance of different plants or habitats; and there was no basis for predicting what density of deer a particular area of ground might support. Equally little was known of the effects of deer density on breeding success and survival, or of the ways in which deer numbers were regulated in the absence of human intervention. As a result, deer management was a hit-or-miss affair based more on tradi-tion and guesswork than on scientific estimates of the annual cull which populations could support.

Studies on Rum by Nature Conservancy scientists in the years fol-lowing the acquisition of the island changed all that, providing the first firm basis for deer management. Rum provided an open-air laboratory where questions about the ecology of the land and its animals and plants could be investigated, and where the requirements of sport were sub-servient to those of scientific research. The Nature Conservancy stopped the practice of regular burning of parts of the moorland to provide fresh growth, and all the sheep and cattle were withdrawn (see CHAPTER 7). Predators were rare, and deer numbers would be limited only by food availability and management by people. To all intents and purposes, the island was left to the self-contained population of 1,600 red deer.

Ageing

Pat Lowe, one of the Nature Conservancy scientists, led the early research effort into the red deer on Rum. One of the first programmes was to develop a reliable means of measuring the ages of the animals. He demonstrated that tooth eruption and wear could provide an accurate basis for measuring age. With this technique he was able to establish the ages of animals culled or dying naturally on the island, and to draw up the first life-table for red deer – a quantitative summary of the breeding success and survival of the average red deer in each year of its lifespan.

One of the results of his work was to put paid to the traditional idea that red deer are very long-lived: 'Thrice the age of a dog is that of a horse, thrice the age of a horse is that of a man, thrice the age of a man is that of a deer'. In fact, few stags live for more than thirteen years, and few hinds for more than fifteen–even in populations which are not culled. Another was to provide a basis for calculating the size of the annual cull which the population could sustain. The Scottish Committee of the Nature Conservancy decided that this should be 100 stags and 140 hinds – around 16% of the spring population; and this figure is still widely quoted. The Committee hoped that this would reduce the population to around 300 animals; in practice, however, the numbers went up rather than down! Pat Lowe argued that this fixed figure of 16% was too low for Rum, and too inflexible, and suggested that the population could support a total cull of 20%, although the discrete deer populations on the island could support different levels of culling. Later researchers have suggested that, when weather conditions are unfavourable, culls of only 11% can be large enough to limit the size of the population.

Food

Another group of Nature Conservancy scientists, led by Nigel Charles, measured the extent to which the deer utilised different plant communities. Perched in a hut on top of Orval they plotted the distribution of grazing deer on different types of vegetation in the vast scoop of Guirdil, checking their results against analyses of deer faeces. One of the main results of this work was to show the extent to which deer depended on small patches of 'sweet' grazing dominated by meadow-grass, fescues and herbs (although plant communities of this kind cover less than 5% of the island), and how little they used the moorland communities dominated by heather, purple moor-grass and deer sedge.

Exclosures to prevent grazing were established, in order to investigate the impact of deer and the rate of woodland regeneration when they were excluded; thirty years later, these suggested that grazing has a role in maintaining the diversity of plant species – the smaller plots from which deer were excluded lost more than 75% of their species, and showed little evidence of the reappearance of natural woodland (in some parts of Rum, at least).

Hummels

Leading up to, and following, the reorganisation of the Nature Conservancy into the Nature Conservancy Council in 1973, many of its scientists moved to the new and independent Institute of Terrestrial Ecology (ITE), and their work focused more and more on mainland deer populations. This provided an opportunity for a university-based research group from Cambridge to use the unique facilities which Rum offered, developing collaborative research programmes with the NCC and, later, SNH. Roger Short and Gerald Lincoln from the Veterinary School at Cambridge investigated the hormonal controls of antler growth and shedding. One offshoot of their work examined the contentious issue of whether or not 'hummels' (antlerless adult stags) produced sons lacking antlers; if they did, this would make it important to eliminate them before they bred. A hummel was imported from the mainland and mated to red deer hinds at Kinloch. His sons produced normal antlers and, when these sons were mated with their sisters, the male offspring still showed normal antler growth. Hummelling appears to have no simple genetic basis and may be caused by unfavourable conditions which affect early development, so there is little to fear from the appearance of an occasional hummel.

Life-histories

One limitation of the early work on the ecology of red deer was that it was not possible to recognise individual deer throughout their lifespan. Right from the start, Pat Lowe and his colleagues had pursued a widespread programme of marking and recording hundreds of calves over the whole island, but it was still difficult to measure precisely how widely individual animals ranged, or to tell whether they lived in discrete groups or unstable herds. Their development at different stages of their lifespan could not be related to their subsequent breeding success or survival, nor was it possible to assess the extent to which a parent's age, breeding history or physique affected the growth and survival of its offspring. This was a crucial gap in knowledge, because many aspects of deer management depend on understanding those relationships. If, for example, calves born to old mothers show the best growth and survival, it could be a mistake to cull old hinds even if their fertility was reduced; similarly, unless the antler characteristics of sons are inherited from their fathers, there may be little point in adopting an expensive and time-consuming policy of culling stags with poor antlers.

Research on Rum after 1972 focused more closely on these questions; it was led by Tim Clutton-Brock of the Zoology Department at Cambridge. The Kilmory area, known as the 'North Block' (Deer Management Block 4), began to be used for intensive long-term studies which tracked the life-histories of all individuals regularly using the ground. This meant learning to recognise every single animal in the North Block, in order to monitor the breeding success and survival of each individual in the population. Much of this pioneering observational work was carried out by Fiona Guinness, who until recently lived on the island practically all the year round. By painstakingly recording the behaviour of recognisable animals, the team built up the longest and most detailed records of individual life-histories available for any mammal population anywhere in the world.

The results of research in the North Block confirmed that much of the traditional 'knowledge' of red deer had little basis in fact. For example, it had been thought that hinds which failed to breed in one season and therefore entered the winter in good condition would probably produce the best calves; the Kilmory research showed that, on the contrary, hinds which fail to reproduce one year are more likely to fail to rear offspring in successive years, even if they are in superior body condition (indeed, these 'yeld' hinds, as they are called, were the only hinds culled by the early Nature Conservancy researchers). Similarly, it was the traditional practice to cull old, tatty-looking hinds because it was generally assumed that their calves were unlikely to survive; the Kilmory records showed that this, too, was untrue – old mothers tend to suckle their offspring more frequently and produce a high proportion of the best calves.

The cost of sons

One of the most exciting finds to come out of the North Block research was that sons cost more to rear than daughters. Stag calves are born heavier than hind calves and grow more rapidly. They also demand more milk. As a result, rearing a son reduces the mother's fat reserves more than rearing a daughter, so that hinds which have reared a son are more likely to die in the next winter and, if they survive, are less likely to breed the following year than hinds which have reared a daughter. The sex ratio is adaptive: only the large, dominant mothers who can sustain the high cost of rearing sons produce more sons than daughters, while small subordinate hinds produce more daughters than sons.

To enable these studies to take place, all culling in the North Block was stopped in 1972. As a result, deer numbers there rose rapidly from 180 to about 310 animals. Surprisingly, it was the number of hinds, not stags, which accounted for the increase: the ratio of stags to hinds changed radically, from about one hind to two stags to almost the reverse. It turned out that where the population density is high, competition for food increases – and the hinds win out: they invade areas previously preferred by stags, and the stags are forced to use the poorer grazing areas.

Perhaps the most surprising finding was that rising hind density depressed juvenile survival to a greater extent in males than in females. As hind density rose, the survival of males during their first two years of life fell from around 90% to around 40%, while the survival of females fell from 90% to around only 70%.

Implications for deer management

These findings have substantial implications for the management of red deer populations throughout Scotland. The received wisdom of Victorian sporting estate management was that the more hinds you had on your land, the more stags would be attracted to the area, to be stalked and shot as trophies. The Rum research has shown that the precise opposite is true, and that proper culling of hinds is vital to sustain a healthy stag population. In wild red deer, growth (including antler weight and size) and reproductive success decline with increasing population density and competition for scarce food resources. So hind numbers need to be controlled in order to maximise the annual yield of mature stags: high hind numbers reduce male survival and growth and increase the male emigration rate, thus lowering the number of mature stags which can be shot each year – and therefore lowering the estate income which can be derived from stalking.

Research in the North Block still continues, which is why visitor access to Kilmory is presently restricted at some times of the year. Current work there, involving scientists from the University of Edinburgh and the ITE at Banchory, as well as from Cambridge, is investigating the inheritance of antler characteristics and breeding success in males, the genetic factors affecting survival and breeding success in females, and the effects of climate change on performance and habitat use.

The Deer Commission for Scotland (previously the Red Deer Commission) has always taken a keen interest in the Rum herd and the various studies on it, and has provided valuable assistance with the annual counts. Since 1992 it has been a partner in a new research project on the island, which involves stags and hinds being culled at different levels in separate blocks in order to distinguish between the effects of male and female numbers on the survival and body-condition of hinds and stags, as well as on any changes in the vegetation. The hypothesis is that where hinds are culled heavily, stag condition and survival will improve; and where stags are culled heavily, there will be no impact on either hind or stag condition or survival.

The Rum deer population is also important today because, like some other island stocks, it appears to be one of the few populations which are not directly threatened with hybridisation with sika deer. Sika were introduced to Scotland from Japan in the late 1800's and all but the remoter island populations (some 6% of the Scottish red deer herd) are in danger of hybridisation with sika. Even some of the remoter islands have had red deer introduced recently, some of which may already be sika hybrids. Rum has not had any such introductions since the 1920s, so it possibly possesses one of the purest red deer stocks in Britain, albeit of mixed origin.

What of the future? As a natural part of the island's wildlife, red deer will always have a place on Rum, but with future management more strongly focused on restoring habitats and on sustaining higher levels of biodiversity, their numbers will require to be substantially reduced. This development will offer opportunities to look at controlled change both to the deer population and to the vegetation on which it depends. Research on Rum has already had a massive impact on our knowledge of land mammals, and has earned rich praise in many quarters; it will doubtless continue to have widespread and important implications for deer management.

CHAPTER 12

Ponies, Highland Cattle,
Goats and other Mammals

The Rum ponies

ONE OF THE MOST DELIGHTFUL ASPECTS of 'wildlife' on Rum is the herd of native Rum ponies which add vivid colour and character to the island.

The Rum ponies are smaller than the Highland and Skye ponies: they stand between 13.1 and 13.3 hands. They are thickset and powerfully built, with long thick forelocks, lengthy flowing manes and bushy tails. They come in many colours – black, white, grey, mouse-dun and bay, as well as an attractive chestnut with silver mane and tail ('fox dun'). All the ponies have a dark eel-stripe down their backs, and many have dark zebra markings encircling the forelegs above the fetlocks.

Rum ponies

Where did they come from? Rum ponies are related to those of the Western Isles of Scotland. Some people claim (rather improbably) that they swam ashore from the wrecked ships of the Spanish Armada. Others think that the zebra markings on their forelegs link them with the primitive breeds of northern Europe. They may well be the descendants of the Scandinavian horses which the Norsemen took with them on their colonising expeditions – wonderfully sturdy, docile creatures which cheerfully carried the world on their backs.

The Rum ponies were first mentioned in print by Thomas Pennant in 1772 (*A tour in Scotland and voyage to the Hebrides*), when he referred to:

> an abundance of mares and a necessary number of stallions; the colts are an article of commerce, but *[the inhabitants]* never part with their fillies.

A few years later, Dr Johnson mentioned that Maclean of Coll, the owner of Rum, described the ponies as being 'very small, but a breed eminent for beauty' (*A Journey to the Western Isles of Scotland*, 1775). The *Old Statistical Account* of 1796 reported that horses were reared for sale on Rum, and called them 'hardy and high mettled, though of a small size'.

After the Rum Clearances in the mid-1820s the ponies were left to run wild until the Marquis of Salisbury purchased the island in 1845. One of his sons, Lord Arthur Cecil, took a particular interest in the stud; he described how, in 1862, his father took a number of animals, including stallions, to his own herds at Hatfield, in North London, and in the New Forest. They were all quite wild, but two were eventually broken in by Lord Arthur and his brother Lionel. The two ponies lived to be nearly 30 years old – and even as 20-year-olds they could trot 12 miles (19.3 km) in 55 minutes.

Lord Arthur continued his interest in the ponies while the grazings were let to the Campbells in 1863 (see CHAPTER 4). When the livestock was sold at auction in Oban in 1868, prior to the sale of the island to the Campbells in 1870, Lord Arthur bought a number of the ponies for his programme of improvements to the New Forest stock.

When the Campbells, in turn, sold the island to John Bullough in 1888 and put the livestock to auction in Oban, Lord Arthur added a few more Rum ponies to his New Forest stock. These purchases were particularly fortunate, because they saved the Rum line from breaking up. When George Bullough, who developed a life-long passion for race-horses, inherited Rum from his father in 1891, he was able to re-establish a stud based on the old Rum stock; he bought two mares in foal to Lord Arthur's black Rum stallion, Skye. From then on he sent other mares to England to be covered by Lord Arthur's stallions, but he also brought in stallions to run on Rum, the most notable being Claymore. He wanted to ensure a plentiful supply of sure-footed pack-horses to carry red deer carcasses home from the hill during the stalking season.

According to Archie Cameron, who was born on Rum in 1903 and spent much of his life there (*Bare Feet and Tackety Boots*, 1988), George Bullough also tried to 'improve' the stock by introducing a white pure-bred Arab stallion:

> The 'improvement' certainly produced some remarkable colours, such as various shades of cream and gold with chestnut manes and tails and vice versa. The Rum ponies are not therefore a strain unadulterated since the time of the Norsemen's occupation of the Western Isles as is often claimed, but it is to their credit that they have been able to revert to the appearance and characteristics of the breed despite dilution over many generations of their forebears.

By the 1930s there were 26 ponies in the stud; after the death of Sir George Bullough in 1939, his widow continued to maintain the herd. No new mares were introduced, so the lines established at the turn of the century are still extant today.

When the Nature Conservancy acquired the island in 1957, its Land Agent for Scotland, John Arbuthnott, developed a different breeding policy to strengthen the integrity of the herd. He borrowed, from the New Calgary stud in Sussex, a Western Isles stallion bred from the old Calgary strains on Mull – the first link with the Hebridean stock for some time.

There are currently 17 ponies in the Rum stud, with a good age-range and sex ratio. The main herd stays out on the hill during the year, mainly in Kilmory Glen and Kinloch Glen, with only the pregnant mares and the foals being pastured in Kinloch during the winter.

Pride of place has always gone to the reigning stallion. At present he is a superb 12-year-old called Silver Fox Snowstorm ('Storm' for short), which was bought in 1994 from owners in the West Country; his sire was a full Rum pony called Rum Hallival. He has the classic Rum markings and the ultimate colouring of silver fox dun with silver mane and tail. He has a mind of his own, has Storm, like all good Vikings. He needs firm handling, and a congenial companion – a seven-year-old gelding called Rum Fjall, known as 'Norman', who is prepared to stand up to Storm's occasional temper. Norman is also one of the best stalking ponies on Rum, along with another seven-year-old called Duke.

The mares are the mainstay of the herd. They were all born and bred on Rum and can both work and breed vigorously. Norma I is 28 years old and still going strong, supported by Primrose III (19), Norma II (15) and Beth I (14). There is a younger generation (4-9 years old) growing up which is now gaining experience both in the field and on the hill; their colours vary from an attractive dark liver dun (Fionchra) to light grey (Becky) and mouse dun (Mary IV).

Storm has several years to go on Rum, but has already secured the future of the stud by siring three fillies in the last two years. It would be ideal if his future offspring were to include some colts which could be sold intact to boost Rum blood on the mainland.

Meanwhile, it is not inconceivable that one day the ponies of Rum will develop an additional role in addition to their historical and cultural links with the island: as trekking ponies for future visitors.

Highland Cattle

Mention the word 'Scotland' anywhere in the world, and what do people say? They say 'wonderful scenery'. They say 'golden eagles'. They say 'red deer, the monarchs of the glen'. But they also say 'Highland cattle'. Like the golden eagle and the stag at bay, the Highlander is considered a totem of wild Scotland. Highland cattle certainly *look* the part – shaggy and formidably horned; but underneath that rough exterior they are docile, durable, hardy, good-natured, easy to handle, long-suffering, fecund and immensely lovable.

What makes a good Highlander? James Macdonald, in his *General*

View of the Agriculture of the Hebrides (1811), had this to say:

> His colour should be black (that being reckoned the hardiest and most durable species), or dark brown or reddish brown...His head should be rather small, his muzzle fine, his eyes lively and prominent, his horns equable, not very thick, of a clear, green and waxy tinge; his neck should rise with a gentle curve from his shoulders, and should be small and fine where it joins the head; his shoulders moderately broad at the top, joining full to his chine and chest backwards and to the vane of his neck forwards. His bosom should be open, his breast broad, and projecting well before his legs; his arms or fore-thighs muscular and tapering to the knee; his legs straight, well covered with hair, and strong boned... His general appearance should combine agility, vivacity and strength; and his hair should be glossy, thick and vigorous, indicating a sound constitution and perfect health.

The Highlander is as much a part of the cultural heritage as anything else – and perhaps even more central to it, because it has not been *imposed* on the land like many other creatures: it is grown out of the land itself, as it were. It is an animal which was raised on farms in the Highlands and Islands where there were minimal arable opportunities, a breed which was an integral part of its environment.

The animal has a remarkable ability to survive on poor herbage and is therefore ideally suited to certain kinds of west coast farming areas. Over the centuries it has evolved the characteristics which enable it to thrive on the storm-swept environments of the Highlands and Islands. It has learned how to forage and to utilise those areas on which other stock can barely exist. It possesses a body metabolism (in paticular concerning fat deposi-

Highland cow; Bloodstone Hill in the background

tion), and low heat-loss through its coat, which other 'improved' breeds do not have. It can pluck vegetation by pulling it out of the ground (it is not a 'mowing machine' like sheep), hence its importance in managing tall, rough, rank vegetation. So its value, quite apart from its potent symbolism, is that it can be used as a manager on some of the more inhospitable parts of the natural heritage.

Once the sheep and cattle had been removed from Rum in 1957, in order to allow heavily over-grazed parts of the island to recover, red deer and feral goats were the only herbivores left. For the next ten years, Nature Conservancy staff monitored with great care 13 vegetation plots of different types across the island. The results showed that species-rich plant communities were being replaced by species-poor communities. A few aggressive species were producing rough tussocks. Deer (and the 180 feral goats) were avoiding these areas. In sum, because of the reduced grazing pressure, detrimental changes were occurring in the species composition.

In 1971 John Morton Boyd, the new Director (Scotland) of the Nature Conservancy, took the decision to re-introduce Highland cattle in order to improve the grazing neglected by the red deer. The first group of 13 young cattle, purchased from various sources, were shipped from Mallaig in May 1971. Their journey was an eventful one. When the cattle float arrived in Mallaig it couldn't get down to the landing-craft, so the animals were let out just to the north of town. The young cattle, all from different folds, had their own distinctive characteristics; some were quiet and docile, others were much wilder. No sooner were they out of the float than they scattered, and rounding them all up was a hectic and difficult job. The Mallaig rodeo which ensued is still remembered with some awe in those parts.

When the beasts eventually reached Rum they were released near Harris. By careful management in the early months they gelled into a fold of their own, and became hefted to Harris. The numbers have built up, and now fluctuate between 30 and 50.

The wisdom of the decision to re-introduce Highland cattle to Rum has become clearer and clearer: the experiment on Rum has demonstrated convincingly that putting Highland cattle into certain areas has helped to keep down large tussocks of purple or tufted moor-grass, for instance, which were swamping other vegetation. In their place we have seen a much greater richness and diversity of flora like wild thyme, kidney vetch, sweet vernal grass and red fescue. So the new grazing regime of red deer and Highland cattle combined has had a beneficial effect on the species composition of some of the herbaceous vegetation communities.

The Highlanders remain on the hill throughout the year, and are only moved away from Harris to Guirdil, on the west coast, during July and August. The stock bull – at present a five-year-old called Tòsgaire of Glengorm, from a fold on Mull – is kept within the farm fields at Kinloch for most of the year, but ranges with the majority of the fold on the hill during those two summer months.

The Highlanders on Rum are maintained and managed as a pedigree herd, and are a recognised Highland fold. From the documentation, it is clear that the traditional colour for Highland cattle was black; the Victorians tended to favour the subsidiary reddish colour, and much of their breeding policy was designed to achieve this. The general policy for the Rum fold is to try to increase the numbers of black beasts, although it is not the intention to lose the variety of other colours – the yellows, oranges and browns as well as the reds.

The goats on Rum

Ponies and Highland cattle are genuine and tangible links to the indigenous people of Rum, for whom they were a necessary part of farming life. So, too, are the multi-coloured wild goats on the island. About 200 of them frequent the rocky crags and sea-cliff pastures on the coastal strip between Kilmory, Harris and Dibidil; the billies can often be seen silhouetted proudly against a craggy skyline as they survey their realm.

The goats have been there for a very long time – and they used to be of considerable commercial value to the islanders. John Walker recorded (*Report on the Hebrides of 1764 and 1771*):

> There is a great Number of Goats kept upon the Island, and here I found an Article of Oeconomy generally unknown in other Places. The People of Rum carefully collect the Hair of their Goats, and after sorting it, send it to Glasgow where it is sold from 1 shilling to 2 shillings and 6d. per pound according to its fineness, and there it is manufactured into Wigs, which are sent to America.

These domestic goats may well have become feral soon afterwards, and since then there have been occasional 'escapes' of domestic animals no longer wanted by their owners.

Wild goat

The sporting owners of Rum recognised their value for stalking, and in the early 1900s attempts were made by Sir George Bullough to improve the more desirable (i.e. sporting) characteristics of the stock – notably the size and shape of the horns – from Perthshire goats, with numbers supplemented later from Sunart in Argyll. Their influence is still evident among the billies, where two completely different horn shapes can be seen: the wide-spreading 'dorcas' type and the closer-set backward-sweeping 'ibex' type. Rum billies acquired a substantial reputation as trophies due to the size of their horns and their unusually dense coats.

When the Nature Conservancy acquired the island in 1957, it was feared that the goats might be a threat to its alpine and coastal flora, and the initial Management Plan recommended a substantial reduction in the goat population – from 185 to 25. It was easier said than done. Despite heavy culling over a number of years the goat population remained stubbornly constant (the nannies kid twice a year, in January and in August). Later it was realised that the coastal vegetation was relatively stable despite the browsing by the goats, so culling was reduced, and the population has stabilised at around 200.

There can be few more spectacular sights than billies fighting during the rut – the ferocity and violence with which they hurl themselves at one another as they battle for supremacy, the strength and courage with which they withstand the thunderous charges and counter-charges. Malodorous they may be, but their presence on the island adds a dimension of natural and heroic vigour.

Other mammals

There are remarkably few species of wild mammals on Rum, due mainly to its having been an island since the last Ice Age. True native land mammals are restricted to the otter and the pipistrelle bat, which could cross the Minch unaided. There are no rabbits or hares (despite efforts to introduce them for sport in 1916); no carnivores other than otters and seals; and no hedgehogs, voles, house mice, moles, squirrels or roe deer.

Otters are common round the coast and along rivers and burns, particularly at Kilmory, Samhnan Insir and Loch Scresort, and breed all around the island. The Loch Scresort Heritage Trail (see CHAPTER 15) goes through a favoured otter area, where the kits can often be seen at play in the early mornings. Otters have frequented that coastline for many centuries; a Gaelic place-name there is Càrn nan Dòbhrain Bhig, meaning 'Cairn of the Little Otter'. The otters seldom penetrate far inland, although tracks have been found at 460 metres on Hallival.

Otter

Pipistrelle bats, the commonest of the British bats, are resident in Kinloch, where they roost in the roofs of buildings like the White House and Lion Cottage: a 1986 survey found some 200 of them, mainly female. Sightings of single bats have also been recorded at Dibidil and Kilmory.

The **field mouse** is found in most parts of the island, including the summit of Hallival. It used to be known as the 'Rum field mouse', *Apodemus hebridensis hamiltoni*, but is no longer thought to be a separate species or sub-species. **Pygmy shrews** are also common and widespread.

The other widespread small mammal on Rum is the **brown rat**, which is found in most places, especially around the coast and in inhabited areas during the winter. They may spread up the hills in summer to breed: young have been seen on the top of Orval in June. In winter snow, tracks have even been spotted 275 metres up on Ard Nev.

CHAPTER 13

Insect Life

IT IS SAID that in the old pre-crofting days a particularly unpleasant form of punishment for wrong-doers in the Small Isles was to strip them naked, tie them to a stake, and leave them exposed in the sun to be bitten to distraction or even death by the midges. Whether the story is apocryphal or not, the viciousness and aggressiveness of the Rum midges on warm, moist summer evenings have to be experienced to be believed. Between May and September the midges swarm in unimaginable numbers and can make outdoor work or leisure of any kind a torment.

Edwin Waugh, who recounted the story in his book *The Limping Pilgrim, on his Wanderings* (1883), proved that one thing at least hasn't changed:

> I spent the whole of last June upon the island, and during the greater part of that time the air swarmed with stinging insects; and their vindictiveness was something startling. They came down in murderous hordes upon every exposed bit of skin about you...

There is also an abundance of clegs (horse-flies) *Haematopota* spp., of which two species occur: *H. crassicornis*, which is northern in distribution, and the very similar *H. pluvialis*, which is generally more abundant in southern England. They, too, are persistent in their pursuit of warm-blooded animals, but compared with the biting midges they are more of a nuisance than an unmitigated pest. Another little fiend to beware of is the sheep tick, which lurks in ambush on the grass of otherwise inviting flowery knolls.

Given the generally inhospitable nature of Rum's climate and terrain, the island would not be expected to support a rich insect fauna. However, it now boasts a catalogue of 2,460 species of insects – 10% of the British total, and over 17% of the Scottish total. This probably reflects the intensity of collecting effort over the years: since Rum became a National Nature Reserve it has become the most fully documented of any Scottish offshore island, although each new survey brings to light further additions to the list.

Small pearl-bordered fritillary

The earliest published records of insects on Rum were of water beetles, collected in 1884 by a visiting botanist, Symington Grieve. A whiff of academic scandal hangs over the first major work on the island's insects, however. It was carried out by Professor J Heslop-Harrison of Durham University, who led regular expeditions to the island between 1938 and 1957. He concentrated his efforts on botanical surveys, but he also collected information on butterflies and moths, beetles, and gall-making insects which included flies, aphids and gall wasps. Many of the insects he recorded were subsequently confirmed from the localities in which he found them, but the problem for both plants and insects was that a few spectacular rarities have never been seen on Rum again, and serious doubts have been expressed about the authenticity of his records – particularly the large blue butterfly, which is now extinct in Britain (but was recently reintroduced in south-west England by English Nature), and the slender Scotch burnet moth. Some of these more unusual records, it is suspected, may have been mischievously introduced.

Since 1960, Rum's invertebrates have been the subject of regular study. From 1960-63 intensive surveys (by W O Steel and G E Woodroffe) produced a baseline list of 1,722 species. More species were added by further surveys led by Steel, as well as independent contributions from several visiting entomologists and resident staff; these were collated and published by Peter Wormell, the Warden/Naturalist on Rum from 1957-73, in 1982. This was the first proper catalogue of species for the island, and it included many interesting records: for example, no fewer than 10 species of aphids, none of which had been recorded in Scotland before, were found on Rum in 1969 – three of them 'firsts' for the British Isles.

There is space here to give only a flavour of the range and importance of Rum's invertebrates.

Butterflies and moths (Lepidoptera)

The most visible and vivid – and the most intensively surveyed – of the insect species are the butterflies and moths (Lepidoptera). A total of 504 have been found; 19 of these are butterfly species, of which 11 are resident breeders. The commonest butterfly on the island, abundant over heathland and grasslands up to 300 metres, is the small heath, while the large heath is locally common on the moors and strongly associated with bogs, where its foodplant, the cottongrass, grows. The large dark meadow brown is also common over grasslands and drier grassy heathland. The small pearl-bordered fritillary is characteristic of moorland, as is the striking dark green fritillary and its sub-species, *scotica*, whose females are suffused with dark green, almost black, scales on the upper side.

The only woodland butterfly is the speckled wood, which has been established at Kinloch since 1946 and is abundant in other woodlands.

The orange tip caused excitement when a migrant male or males appeared on Rum in the summer of 1992, because this species colonised western Inverness-shire in the late 1980s and northern Argyll in 1990. They are now firmly established on the Benderloch peninsula in Argyll, and could well gain a foothold and form a resident population in the Inner Hebrides. Meanwhile the grayling, with its superb lichen-like camouflage, which is declining in its inland habitats, continues to hold its own on Rum on rocky outcrops by the shore and on the sand dunes.

Among the most abundant moths of the moorland habitat on Rum are the fox, the drinker, the northern eggar and the emperor, all of whose caterpillars feed on heather and other dwarf shrubs and provide a steady diet for the island's large spring and summer population of cuckoos.

Some of the moths on Rum have local forms. The wings of the Edinburgh pug, for instance, are very heavily and distinctively patterned and may represent a distinct sub-species.

The belted beauty is nationally rare but the wingless females can be seen laying their eggs on lichen-covered rocks or pieces of driftwood near the beach at Kilmory; the males are handsome creatures with grey and white striped wings, and they fly in the early evening from one female to another. The spectacular red and dark-green transparent burnet, whose larvae feed on wild thyme on sunny south-facing scree slopes near the coast, is also nationally rare and is confined to the Inner Hebrides and Argyll. The six-spot burnet is common and widely distributed across the island.

A rare upland moth is *Scrobipalpa murinella*, whose larvae mine the leaves of alpine everlasting. Another unusual species is the nationally scarce grass moth *Catoptria furcatellus*, which on Rum is confined to the high-level grasslands fertilised by the shearwater colonies on Hallival.

Another two nationally scarce species are found in lightly-grazed unimproved grasslands: the slender striped rufous and the narrow-bordered bee hawk.

The magpie, which normally lives on currant or gooseberry bushes elsewhere, has adapted to moorland conditions on Rum, where it feeds on heather; it is so abundant that thousands of its caterpillars fall into streams and pools from rank, overhanging heather to provide a feast for brown trout. The grey inhabits the coastal cliffs in the south and west of the island; it is a nationally rare species, confined to Argyll and the Inner Hebrides.

Dragonflies (Odonata)

The recent dragonfly atlas for the UK shows 11 (or 12) species with records from Rum, although the record for the nationally rare northern emerald *Somatochlora arctica* is very old. All the dragonfly species are moorland species, and are typical of the west Highlands and Islands. The Odonata comprise four damselflies (the blue-tailed, the common blue, the emerald and the large red) and six dragonfly species (the azure hawker, the black darter, the common hawker, the four-spotted chaser, the gold-ringed dragonfly and the northern emerald). A darter of the genus *Sympetrum* is also recorded, which is probably the Highland darter, but the common darter may be present as well.

The most notable is the scarce azure hawker, which breeds in peaty pools with sphagnum moss around the margins. A small pool behind the raised beach at Harris, which is strongly influenced by salty spray, supports a surprisingly large number of them.

Beetles (Coleoptera)

There are 523 species of beetles: about a third of them are staphylinids (burying, carrion and rove beetles) and carabids (tiger and ground beetles). Among the mountain species are the predatory ground beetles *Leistus montanus* and *Amara quenseli*, which live on open stony areas and are nationally scarce. Another nationally scarce ground beetle, *Elaphrus uliginosus*, lives in marshy places and on loch margins. On the mud flats an uncommon rove beetle, *Arena tabida*, lives under stones in coastal sand.

The policy woods at Kinloch now support a good range of woodland beetles such as the pine weevil and several species of bark- and wood-boring beetles. A featherwing beetle, *Ptinella limbata*, lives under bark in dead parts of trees. Only one species of longhorn beetle is represented, *Asemum striatum*, which breeds in pine-stumps; it appeared in the Kinloch woodlands in the 1960s and is now well established. As the woodland develops, we can confidently predict that further species of woodland beetles will colonise the island; it is surprising what a pair of wings, assisted by the wind, can accomplish!

Ladybirds are very scarce, with only two species; one of them is *Coccinella undecimpunctata*, which feeds on the aphids on the herb-rich links behind the dunes at Kilmory.

The water beetles of Rum are also predominantly found in the uplands. The largest of these is *Dytiscus semisulcatus*, whose voracious larvae prey on the tadpoles of the only amphibian present on Rum, the palmate newt.

Ants, wasps, bees, sawflies, ichneumon flies and allied insects (Hymenoptera)

There are 7 species of ant, 9 hunting and true wasps, and 12 bees; the remainder of the hymenoptera consists of sawflies, gall wasps and 189 parasitic wasps, of which one, a Pteromalid, was hitherto undescribed and was named *Coelopisthia caledonia* from a specimen collected on Hallival. These numbers are small, and undoubtedly a thorough search would yield many more species.

There are 18 species of sawflies; one of them, *Monoctenus juniperi*, which feeds on juniper, has been recorded previously in only one other locality in Britain, in Strathspey. Woodland sawflies which rely on particular trees and shrubs are well ensconced, and the giant woodwasp is also firmly established; this is an insect of coniferous forests whose ovipositor consists of a highly efficient drill so that it can lay its eggs deep into solid timber. With its wasp colours, and that 2 cm ovipositor looking like a giant 'sting', it is rather an alarming creature on first sight.

Its parasite is the largest of all British ichneumon flies, the persuasive burglar. It's a fascinating creature. It is equipped with an even more elaborate flexible drilling ovipositor than that of its host, and is able to locate a woodwasp larva and drill down through wood into its feeding tunnel. Then, using its ovipositor as a sting to immobilise the woodwasp larva, it lays a thin worm-like egg alongside it. This larva, on hatching, bores into the woodwasp larva and feeds internally, devouring it in a very short time.

Other insects and arthropods

This chapter does not purport to be a comprehensive account of the invertebrate life on Rum. There is no mention of many 'others', like spiders (of which there are at least 72 species) or grasshoppers and their allies (four of the five common species on Scottish islands have been recorded); surprisingly, the common earwig has not been recorded on Rum.

But there is one creature which is now a world first for Rum – a very special kind of flea. It is the pale-coloured flea *Ceratophyllus fionnus*, which was first collected by Peter Wormell and the late George M Dunnet from Manx shearwater nests on Hallival. This is a very important record: there are no records to date of this species from any other shearwater colony, not even from Canna or Eigg. The flea was described by Professor Michael B Usher, the Chief Scientist of Scottish Natural Heritage, in the *Entomologist's Gazette* (Vol 19). Since the colour of the flea is paler than that of closely related species, it was given the specific name *fionnus*, which is derived from the Gaelic adjective *fionn*, meaning 'pale' or 'white'; but those in the know also recognise it as being derived from 'Fionna', which is the name of Michael Usher's wife.

CHAPTER 14

The Surrounding Seas

PART OF RUM'S ISLAND APPEAL is its marine life. For the visitor to Rum, the ferry-crossing from Mallaig or Arisaig is constantly enlivened by the sight of seabirds and sea mammals. From April to September every moment has its seabirds (see CHAPTER 10) – Manx shearwaters, fulmars, guillemots, razorbills, puffins and shags galore. Harbour porpoises and minke whales frequent the coast of Eigg and the Sound of Rum. Groups of up to 100 common dolphins, white-beaked dolphins, Risso's dolphins and occasional bottlenose dolphins are sometimes spotted in the Sounds of Rum and Canna.

The **harbour porpoise** is the smallest and most widespread cetacean in the UK. It has a characteristic short blunt head with no forehead or beak, and rarely leaps out of the water; usually the only view is of a dark grey back with a small central triangular dorsal fin. The **common dolphin** is the most agile and animated of the dolphins, and can often be seen breaching and bow-riding boats. It has a low, tapering forehead with a distinctively long and slender beak, sometimes white-tipped, and a slender sickle-shaped or straight dorsal fin in the middle of its back. The **white-beaked dolphin**, much larger, has a sloping head with a short, thick and often white beak; it has a large, erect and strongly sickle-shaped dorsal fin in the centre of the back, and is white on the flanks and on the back behind the dorsal fin. **Risso's dolphin** is the largest of the three (2.8-3.3 metres), and has a pale, blunt, rounded head with no beak. It has a relatively tall sickle-shaped dorsal fin, as well as characteristic black and white pencil-like scratches behind the head towards the dorsal fin. The **bottlenose dolphin**, which has no flank markings, is less agile than the common dolphin but often breaches and bow-rides.

Minke whale

The lucky visitor may also be treated to the sight of a **killer whale**, which is an infrequent visitor to these waters. It is most often found in pods of up to six, usually a bull and cows with young. It is easy to identify with its conspicuously black-and-white coloration and the bull's tall triangular dorsal fin (sometimes tilted forward) and conically-shaped head. **Minke whales**, the most common, are regularly sighted passing close in to the island's coastline, particularly in the late summer and autumn.

Only the very occasional **basking shark** is sighted nowadays, alas, reflecting an apparent general decline in their numbers. This remarkable animal, which is the second largest fish in the world and can grow to more than 10 metres long, used to be seen in large numbers in the Sound of Canna.

The waters around Rum support small numbers of both common and grey seals. **Common seals** regularly occupy Loch Scresort and can often be seen basking on the sand flats exposed at low water. They breed there, too; the pups are born in June and swim off the shore with their mothers on the first incoming tide. Some 15-20 **grey** (Atlantic) **seal** pups are born each year in September and October on the rocky shores mainly between Harris and Papadil in the south-west corner of the island. The pups have a white infant coat and are nursed for about three weeks before going to sea to fend for themselves.

The undersea world

The basic foodstuff all marine life depends upon is plankton, whose name is derived from a Greek word meaning 'that which is made to wander or drift': microscopic creatures of many different species, both plants and animals, the bottom of the food-chain, on which all other marine life relies for survival. The smaller species are consumed by the larger, right up to the bigger carnivores, the seals, the whales, the squids and octopuses, and the seabirds – except the mighty basking shark, which eats nothing but plankton. All the sea-floor and pelagic invertebrates depend on plankton as well. The plankton is in two forms – phytoplankton and zooplankton: the phytoplankton is the 'pasture' of the sea which is 'grazed' by the zooplankton in increasing sizes along the food chain to larger denizens of the deep, notably herring, mackerel, sprats and sand-eels. They are still there, but controversial human exploitation of species like the herring and the sand-eel for instance, has helped to push them to the edge of extinction locally.

It is an astonishing world, the realm of undersea. Marine biologists distinguish its provinces as the 'inter-tidal' or 'littoral' (the shore between the highest and lowest tides) and 'sub-tidal' or 'sub-littoral' (the seabed which extends downwards from the mark of the lowest tides).

The **inter-tidal** of Rum is a wonderful mixture of marine habitats. A great variety of bedrock, boulder and sediment is present on the shores which are exposed to prevailing winds and seas from all directions. Add to that the oscillations of the tide and the effects of freshwater run-off, and you get the most diverse set of environmental factors imaginable.

The sheltered shores of Loch Scresort support a wide range of bivalve molluscs including the edible cockle, the sand gaper and the striped Venus. Towards the bottom of this shore there are large numbers of the sand mason worm whose presence is revealed by the dwarf forest of delicately crafted tubes, each with a crown of tentacles made out of sand grains. In the estuaries of the rivers there is a range of fresh and brackish water habitats which are attractive to sea trout.

At the extremity of the tidal range, beneath the surface of the sand in Loch Scresort, the razor-shell (also known as a 'spoot' because of the tell-tale fountain of water it ejects as it burrows into the sand) is found in large numbers beneath the sand; it is a prized delicacy which is increasingly being exploited in many areas of Scotland.

The **sub-tidal** waters around Rum include the rocky bed of the Hebridean shelf, which is masked by sediments deposited by past glaciers and past and present rivers flowing westward from the mainland plateau. In the most sheltered areas there are fine muds, and in the most exposed there are bare rock and pebbles. The sub-tidal waters are comparatively clear, with sufficient light penetrating to around 30 metres to allow the growth of encrusting red seaweeds.

On the eastern coast of Rum the bedrock extends sub-tidally to only between 5 and 10 metres, giving way to sand which gradually becomes muddier with increasing depth. Off the west coast, steeply sloping bedrock extends to around 10 metres, giving way to shelving bedrock and boulders down to at least 20 metres before the sand and mud take over.

The shallow bedrock areas are dominated by communities which can withstand high exposure to wave action. The most typical are the dense forests of 'tangle', a giant brown seaweed found in shallow waters all around Scotland; its thick stalks are draped with red seaweeds, fluffy white corals and orange featherstars. In deep areas the rock surfaces and crevices are colonised by a variety of sea anemones such as the dahlia anemone, which is the largest anemone to be found on the shore in UK waters; the main column or stalk, which is usually reddish with green markings, often has pieces of shell and gravel attached, making the contracted animal difficult to see. Also in the deeper areas is the brilliantly-coloured *Sagartia elegans*, whose column has white rounded wart-like suckers which become larger and more numerous towards the tentacles; their patterning is a riot of red, brown and orange, and they are often found in clumps of varying colours in crevices and overhangs.

Sunstar

The rocks also support growths of sunstars, and of dead men's fingers (animals with a fine, hairy appearance and erect branching colonies divided into a few blunt 'fingers').

In deeper areas, particularly off the west coast of Rum, the offshore rocky reefs support very large numbers of Devonshire cup coral – a true solitary coral with a brown-white skeleton with many curved ridges; the animal inside varies in colour from red, pink, orange, white, green or brown, with as many as 80 tentacles, each ending in a white or brown blob. They also support several encrusting and erect branching sponges, and the northern sea fan, which is a slender, delicately branching, white horny coral which can grow to more than 20 cm in height. In the sandier areas the edible crab and the scallop are common; in the deeper parts there is an eerie forest of sea pens – strange animals, related to the sea anemone, which look like white feathers, two metres or more high, growing out of the deep mud. The muddy seabed is also perforated by the burrows of the Norway lobster, which is the main ingredient of the popular dish scampi for which there is an active fishery in the Sound of Canna and elsewhere around the Small Isles.

Survey

John Morton Boyd, who was Director (Scotland) of the Nature Conservancy and, later, the Nature Conservancy Council from 1970-85, was fond of quoting one of his former ecology tutors at Glasgow University, C M Yonge:

> The sea shore is the meeting place of sea and land: it is for that reason the most fascinating and the most complex of all the environments of land.

As a National Nature Reserve, Rum depends upon its surrounding sea. Its climate is strongly maritime, and its plants and animals are adapted to such conditions. Equally, the sea depends on the land: the lack of large sediment-carrying rivers, or of pollution sources, aids the clarity of the water and the purity of the marine environment.

A comprehensive survey and classification of Rum's marine environment is long overdue. Rum does not have any exceptional claims to marine species rarity, but it is important because it is a largely natural system within a distinct geographical area, and the species and habitats present are representative of the Scottish west coast.

There have been only two, limited sub-littoral marine surveys of the island and its surrounding waters: the first was by Glasgow University Exploration Society, which conducted two dives in Loch Scresort in 1974; the second, in 1980, was a NCC survey which covered all the Small Isles and included 21 dives on sub-littoral sites around Rum; it concluded that Rum had a low species diversity and low diversity of rocky shore habitats compared to the other Small Isles. To date there has been no organised survey of the inter-tidal areas of the coast of Rum, although Professor John Allan, former director of the University Marine Biological Station at Millport, made some initial observations of three inter-tidal areas (Harris, Kinloch and Kilmory) during a visit to the island in 1986; in contrast to the earlier survey, he declared that the head of Loch Scresort represented 'the richest inter-tidal sand beach the observer had ever seen.'

The technology for full-scale survey is now available. There have been great advances in scuba diving, although it is still constrained by the limitations of human physiology – scuba divers are unable to dive safely to depths much greater than 40 metres, and at such depths they can remain on the seabed for only ten minutes. The area of seabed which a diver can cover is also very limited, so the data gathered by diver surveys are specific to isolated spots.

Advances in remote sensing techniques enable much more comprehensive maps of the seabed communities and habitats to be compiled, using techniques such as side-scan sonar and other acoustic ground discrimination systems which measure a reflection of sound from the seabed; when these reflections are analysed they give a measure of the physical nature of the seabed. The biological characteristics of the seabed can then be assessed by visual inspection using a Remote Operated Vehicle (ROV) with a video camera. ROVs have a number of advantages over scuba divers: they can operate at much greater depths (in excess of 300 metres), they can stay submerged for any length of time and they provide a permanent record of life on the seabed and in the water column. Such a video record illustrates, as nothing else can, the true wonders of our marine natural heritage.

There are many opportunities for incorporating the marine and coastal environment into education plans for the island. The Loch Scresort Heritage Trail from Kinloch (see CHAPTER 15) could include interpretation of coastal species (plant, invertebrate, bird and mammal), and a special focus on the inter-tidal aspect when the tide is right (a couple of hours either side of low water). Wildlife cruises could provide visitors to the area with a 'marine' view of Rum, with birds, seals and cetaceans as a focus. Ferry passengers could be regaled with a video about the marine environment they are traversing. Even an 'underwater dive trail', such as the one at the voluntary Marine Nature Reserve at St Abbs, could be established on Rum once further surveys have identified the most interesting sub-tidal areas.

The marine environment has been sadly neglected in research programmes in the past. It is time to put that right.

CHAPTER 15

Accommodating Visitors

The Forbidden Isle

FOR MORE THAN 100 YEARS, Rum was known as 'the Forbidden Isle' because of its exclusive use as a sheep-walk or a sporting estate by its owners from 1845 to 1957. Access from the mailboat to the island was by private boat, and it offered neither welcome nor accommodation for the uninvited visitor.

In the late summer of 1934 two adventurous young Scotsmen made a defiant visit by canoe to the Forbidden Isle, just to prove it could be done. One was Alastair Dunnett, the future editor of *The Scotsman*, then 26 years old; the other was his friend Seumas Adam. The two friends had been involved in an ambitious but ill-fated publishing venture – a twopenny weekly Scottish adventure paper for boys called the *Claymore*, which foundered in July 1934. To console themselves the young men embarked on a spectacular open-sea canoe voyage from the Clyde to the Western Isles. The story of their adventure, and of the social conditions they encountered in the remote west, was first published as *Quest by Canoe: Glasgow to Skye* (Bell, 1950, re-issued in 1996 by Neil Wilson Publishing as *The Canoe Boys*).

As they paddled their perilous way from island to island, people would tell them that they had no hope of landing on Rum. No one was allowed on it without permission. It was common knowledge in yachting, mountaineering and geological circles that visitors were 'not encouraged'. It made them all the more determined, as a matter of principle, to land and spy out this secret land, and to write about it.

Their first attempt to cross the seven miles of the Sound of Rum from Eigg was defeated by fierce winds and heavy seas, and they had to turn and head for shelter on Eigg. On the following day they tried again, and this time they made it into the entrance of Loch Scresort. They landed in the lee of the policy woodlands of Kinloch Castle and were setting up their tent when 'a large man, in tweeds, with a gun and two dogs, arrived scrambling round a shore path and came over to meet us'. He told them that they couldn't stay without permission, but Alastair and Seumas ignored him and carried on pitching their tent, stripping and putting on dry kilts and shoes, and cooking their evening meal.

The man went off, but soon he was back: would they please come and see Lady Bullough? It emerged that Lady Bullough had seen the canoes paddling up the loch and had phoned down to the servants' quarters to report that there were poachers in the loch and that they were not to be allowed to land.

At the Castle, there was a message from Lady Bullough saying that she was sorry but she couldn't see them. However, she gave them permission to camp on the island, and asked them to accept a haunch of venison with her compliments.

That evening they wandered around the little settlement at Kinloch. The islanders were naturally curious about these young kilted strangers who had managed to breach the defences of the Forbidden Isle, and treated them with great hospitality. The haunch of venison was duly delivered to their camp-site next morning; it weighed 26 pounds, and very nearly sank one of their canoes on the six-hour journey across the Sound of Sleat!

When the Nature Conservancy acquired the island in 1957 it issued a statement declaring itself 'a firm supporter of public access', yet severely restricting entry. The general public was to be confined to the Loch Scresort area:

> Visitors without permits will be welcome to land at the Conservancy's pier in Loch Scresort and to visit the Post Office area; but to secure the necessary quiet for scientific experiments and investigations, visitors other than those engaged in the programme of studies will be asked not to range over the remainder of the island.

Only accredited groups of mountaineers from official clubs could visit the Rum Cuillin (Max Nicholson insisted on barring what he called 'the bands of suicide club members infesting so many other Scottish peaks'). In addition, 'naturalists and other visitors able to assist in survey or rehabilitation' could have entry permits for scientific purposes. In fact, no trouble over access ever arose, largely due to the common sense of the Wardens, Peter Wormell and George McNaughton.

The formal attitude adopted by the NCC, and now by SNH, is very different. Over the past 15 years there has been a determined policy not only to admit but to welcome the general public to Rum. There are greater opportunities to visit the island, and the numbers of visitors have grown steadily over the period – almost 10,000 a year now make the journey on the sturdy little Caledonian MacBrayne ferry from Mallaig, the *Lochmor*, or on day-trips on the *Shearwater* from Arisaig.[1]

Those who go to Rum are drawn to the island for all sorts of reasons: there are those who simply wish to enjoy the 'freedom and wildness' of its environment; some are naturalists, eager to contribute to the

---

[1] *At present (1997) the Caledonian MacBrayne ferry Lochmor visits Rum on Mondays, Wednesdays, Fridays and Saturdays all the year round; in summer there are additional day-trips on Wednesdays and Saturdays. The Shearwater from Arisaig makes regular day trips to Rum on Tuesdays and Thursdays during the summer months, with additional sailings on Saturdays and Sundays at the height of the season; these trips usually allow two-to-three hours ashore. The Shearwater is also available for charter.*

enhancement of its natural heritage; others want to explore the history and natural history of a remarkable island phenomenon.

Today, SNH is committed to an open-door policy for Rum, and will continue to develop opportunities for those who wish to enjoy it, contribute to it and learn about it. Rum is a national asset which should be cared for, but it should also be shared and enjoyed. SNH wants to improve public facilities wherever possible, without impinging on the important nature conservation work which is being undertaken there; ultimately, however, visitor numbers have to be managed at levels which the environment of the island can support.

Accommodation

Rum can accommodate 125 visitors overnight in Kinloch, either in the Castle Hostel, or in four bothies, or at the camp-site. Given the restricted accommodation, visitors are expected to book in advance of their arrival on the island. There is a well-stocked General Store and a Post Office. The little whitewashed shop has an off-licence, and serves as an informal al fresco gathering place for the community most evenings.

The Hostel
Kinloch Castle used to be run as a hotel, but at present is only used residentially for special occasions. The servants' quarters behind the Castle have been converted into hostel accommodation, sleeping 30, which is open all the year round. The Hostel offers a choice of self-catering (everything needed is provided in the kitchen), or buying meals in the Castle Bistro, which is open from April to September. Non-resident visitors can also use the Bistro, but are asked to book meals in advance.

The Hostel is much used by educational groups from a wide range of universities and colleges in Britain and further afield, which come to Rum to carry out practical field studies. The Castle also provides a laboratory in the basement, audio-visual facilities, a room for drying wet clothes, and assistance from SNH staff on the island.

Bothies
The Kinloch bothies are converted farm buildings, and are at present run by SNH. They provide basic self-catering accommodation in clean, warm, but rather spartan surroundings, with only a minimum of maintenance by Reserve staff. Each has a gas stove, electricity supply, toilet, shower and kitchen and eating utensils. Visitors bring their own sleeping-bags and pillows, and blankets are available for a small extra charge which covers laundry costs. The four bothies presently in use, which are normally open from March to October, are:

Farmhouse Bothy: 4 bedrooms, to sleep 12.
Stable Bothy: 3 bedrooms, to sleep 8
Stalkers' Bothy: 3 bedrooms, to sleep 8

Foxglove Bothy: 3 bedrooms, to sleep 6.
Smaller groups may have to share accommodation.

There are also two mountain bothies available for public use, at Guirdil and at Dibidil. The **Guirdil** bothy was the shepherd's cottage, built late in the 19th century, and renovated in 1980 by the Mountain Bothies Association in memory of two of the Association's earliest supporters, Tom and Margaret Brown. It's a robust two-roomed bothy with a wooden sleeping platform over one room. The living space is cheerfully decorated with fishing buoys and Rum bloodstone. The **Dibidil** bothy, deep in its glen, is also a renovated, two-roomed shepherd's cottage. They are kept in good repair by dedicated volunteers of the Mountain Bothies Association

These bothies cannot be pre-booked. There is no fee for using them, but a charge is made for accommodation as in the bothies at Kinloch; this ensures that if you are prevented from using the mountain bothies for any reason (such as bad weather), alternative accommodation will still be available for you in the village. There is a maximum stop-over of three nights at either Dibidil or Guirdil; this ensures that they do not become 'long-stay' facilities.

There were three stone-built shooting lodges, at Harris, Kilmory and Papadil, which were used by stalkers in the old days. The lodge at **Harris** is now a bothy used by SNH staff and others on research or survey projects in the south of the island; the **Kilmory** lodge bothy is used by researchers from Cambridge University studying red deer in the 'North Block'. The **Papadil** lodge is now a ruin, alas. It was in relatively good order when the Nature Conservancy acquired the island in 1957; but it was in an extremely remote location, and it was rumoured that it was being regularly used by deer poachers. The Nature Conservancy decided to put it out of commission, and removed the roof.

The Caledonian MacBrayne ferry, *MV Lochmor*

Camping

Camping on Rum is centred on the village of Kinloch. The camp-site starts at the old lime-kiln near the pier and extends round two areas of the Loch Scresort foreshore. Campers can pitch tent anywhere on those areas below the foreshore road. The site has a standpipe water-supply and two public toilets. There are designated areas for wood fires. Some 'wild camping' is permissible beyond the confines of Kinloch, although there have to be controls over the numbers, location and time of year.

On foot on Rum

Day visitors generally have only a few hours to spend ashore before the ferry leaves, but there are opportunities to walk on one of the island Heritage Trails, join a guided tour of Kinloch Castle, and discover more about the history and present-day management of Rum. Whoever comes to Rum, whether for a short break or a longer stay, has the chance of exploring the island with few restrictions on access (imposed only for strictly nature conservation reasons), and there are excellent walking routes for all levels of fitness and experience.

Private vehicles are not allowed on Rum. There is only one road on the island. It is a very rough road indeed – more like a dried riverbed in most places, and fit only for four-wheel drive vehicles. It strikes inland up Kinloch Glen to the centre of the island, where it forks: one branch goes north to Kilmory, and the other south-west to Harris.

In addition to the road, there are a few trackways which were constructed during the last century for stalkers and their ponies; these lead into the more remote western parts of the island, such as Bloodstone Hill, Guirdil from Malcolm's Bridge, and Shellesder from Kilmory Fank, and are a useful foundation for a number of popular walks.

Heritage Trails

There are three Heritage Trails on Rum, all starting from the Information Point beside the Reserve office, where Trail leaflets are available; these should be consulted for fuller accounts of each Trail.

Kinloch Township Heritage Trail (1.5 km, 45 minutes)

The Kinloch Township Trail is a circular walk around the village – an ideal short stroll to complement a tour of the Castle or a visit to the teashop in the Community Centre; it traces the history of the village and the people who have inhabited it. It follows the road from the Reserve office, past the Castle, down the Kinloch River to the Post Office, and returns via the shore road.

Loch Scresort Heritage Trail (5 km out and back, 2 hours)

This Trail goes along the south shore of Loch Scresort; the ground is frequently boggy or rough.

The route goes through the planted trees, past the school house and through the Southside Wood. Insect-eating plants abound. A solitary grave and several old black-houses at Càrn nan Dòbhran (the Otter's Cairn) point to relatively recent settlement, and rough moorland beyond leads to the abandoned settlement of Port nan Carannan, whose ruined cottages are now the home of nesting eider and noisy gulls. Seals and otters may be seen, and snipe heard 'drumming' in the gloaming.

Kinloch Glen Heritage Trail (circular walk of 8 km, about 2 hours)
The Kinloch Glen Trail leads north through the village before crossing the Kinloch River and continues up to one of the large farm fields, before picking up an ancient trackway which leads westwards through Kinloch Glen. It runs parallel to the main Glen road to Kilmory, and was the route which the 'peasantry' used to take (the toffs went along the Glen road).

There are three fields in view, called 'parks', which are very good for ground-nesting birds like curlew and snipe. There aren't many skylarks – they tend to be more on the grassy glens on the western side of the island. Lapwing try to nest here, but tend to be more successful at Kilmory.

The new route opens up the vistas. It gives the impression of being in among the hills without the struggle of going up to the top of them, and gives a good feel for the island as a whole. It's a great half-day taster for the island.

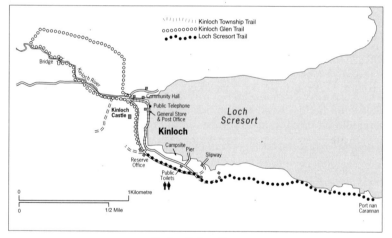

Heritage Trails on Rum

Walks

Kinloch to Harris (10 km each way: 6 hours, including an hour at Harris)
Head up Kinloch Glen until you arrive at a stone bridge below the waterfall, passing, on your right, the 'Rocking Stone'. A kilometre further on, the road divides, the right fork leading to Kilmory. Taking the left fork you see the remains of 'Salisbury's Dam' (see CHAPTER 4).

The track now crosses Stable flats and Malcolm's Bridge, the latter marking the start of a pony-path to Bloodstone Hill and Guirdil. However, your route is straight on, and when the road reaches its highest point you are rewarded with a panoramic view across Loch an Dornabac to the Cuillin of Rum.

As you descend into Harris Bay another fine view opens up, beyond Ardnamurchan point to Mull, the Treshnish Isles, Coll and even (on a clear day) Iona and Tiree.

From Harris you retrace your route to Kinloch. The seasoned walk-er can cross the beach at Harris to find the cliff path to Papadil, Dibidil and eventually round the coasts to Kinloch; but be warned – it is an extremely long and, in places, arduous route.

Kinloch to Coire Dubh (5 km there and back: 2 hours)

The walk up to Coire Dubh, following an old pony-path, is quite short. It starts at the ornamental stone bridge just to the south of the Castle, and follows the Allt Slugan a' Choilich burn. It climbs fairly steeply up to the deer-fence, where it begins to flatten out as the corrie itself is reached. Towards the top, the path skirts a narrow ravine above the Coire Dubh dam which provides the island's power-supply from the hydro-electricity scheme, and also supplies the domestic water for the village; farther on, within the corrie itself, are the remains of an origi-nal dam, which was probably built as a silt-trap to hold back erosion material washed down from the hills.

Kinloch to Dibidil and back (17 km: 7 hours, including an hour at Dibidil)

This walk starts about 50 metres outside the white gates which are to the south of the Reserve office. It is indicated by a way-marker, and leads over the shoulder of one of the low hills which surround Kinloch, fol-lowing an old pony-path which is still used for stalking. Once over the summit you see the most recent stage of the tree-planting programme, with some fine alder, willow and birch on either side of the path. There is a slight descent to the perimeter deer-fence, which has a large gate.

The pony-path runs south along the eastern slopes of Hallival and Askival; as the horizon unfolds there are excellent views of Eigg and Muck and across to the mainland. As the path approaches Dibidil it gets closer to Welshman's Rock and other high sea-cliffs, allowing superb glimpses of nesting gull-colonies and the huge communities of guille-mots and razorbills.

Eventually the path emerges at the bottom end of Glen Dibidil, one of the most dramatically rugged short glens on the island, striking deeply into the steep-walled flanks of Askival on one side and Ainshval and Sgùrr nan Gillean on the other, with Trollaval blocking the head of the glen. The glen itself is full of glacial moraines and steep gullies; at the bottom is the superbly-sited Dibidil bothy, which has been beautifully restored by the Mountain Bothies Association and affords overnight refuge for those wishing to spend more time out among the mountains.

The outward trip from Kinloch takes about three hours, and there are three options for return. You can retrace your steps along the pony-path; you can take the difficult, unmarked route onward via Papadil to Harris and thence by the road to Kinloch; or you can go up Glen Dibidil into the Bealach an Oir ('Pass of the Gold'), between Askival and Trollaval, and follow the contour round the Atlantic Corrie to reach the Barkeval-Hallival pass before descending to Kinloch.

An alternative route for the Kinloch-Dibidil walk is to do this in reverse: to follow the pony-path from Kinloch to Coire Dubh (see *Kinloch to Dibidil, above*), then on to the Bealach an Oir and contouring round (or going over) Hallival and Askival before dropping down to Dibidil and returning via the coast track.

The Cuillin Ridge

The **Cuillin Ridge** offers one of the most attractive of walks on the island, and involves traversing most or all of the principal mountains on the island. The traverse of the main ridges and summits of the Rum Cuillin is rated one of the classic mountain treks in all the Scottish islands outside Skye. It is a wonderful outing for the hill-fit, involving only occasional moderate scrambling and, on a good day, it provides some of the most memorable views of mountain and sea to be found anywhere in Europe.

From Kinloch it takes between 8 and 11 hours. Shorter sections are possible (by omitting Barkeval, for instance).

The classic walk starts from Kinloch and goes up the Coire Dubh along the Allt Slugan a' Choilich burn to the old dam. Here the track forks; you can branch off to the right via Meall Breac ('The Speckled Hill') in order to 'bag' Barkeval, or head for the Bealach Barcabhal ('Barkeval Pass') and turn south-east to ascend the north-west ridge of Hallival. Hallival can look fearsome from below, but once in among the large boulder scree the climb is little more than a mild scramble.

From Hallival the route continues south along a sloping grassy shelf to the north ridge of Askival, the highest summit on Rum, where great care is required to negotiate the unstable scree. Some climbers will want to tackle the knife-edge ('Cathedral Roof') ridge itself, but most people prefer to take the less intimidating east side of the ridge before turning uphill to the summit with its Ordinance Survey column. The panoramic view from the top can be breathtaking, encompassing a great length of the mountainous sea-board and the Inner Hebrides close by, with the Outer Hebrides strung out along the western horizon.

From Askival there is a descent to the Bealach an Oir; be prepared for more scrambling in a direct ascent of Trollaval with its unusual twin-peak topography. The route now descends to the Bealach an Fhuarain ('Pass of the Spring') before a steep haul up a thin zig-zagging path to the cairn on the summit of Ainshval, the second highest peak on Rum. A long grassy ridge gives access to the massive bulk of Sgùrr nan Gillean ('Peak of the Young Men'). From there a long ridge, Leac a' Chaisteil ('The Slab of the Castle') leads west to the summit of Ruinsival, above Harris, thus completing the Ridge Walk. From Ruinsival the route descends through the Fiachanais basin down to the raised beaches of Harris, for the homeward lap along the Land Rover track to Kinloch.

Serious mountaineers are recommended to read Hamish M Brown's helpful and readable booklet, *The Island of Rhum: a Guide for walkers, climbers and visitors* (Cicerone Press, 1995).

Mountain safety

Safety in the hills is a major consideration for visitors to Rum; there have been some fatal and other serious accidents in recent years, unfortunately. On a good day the Cuillin Ridge is a truly magnificent walk; but it has to be planned with care, particularly in terms of time and equipment. People intending to do the Ridge Walk can seek advice at the Reserve Office in Kinloch.

There is a mountain rescue service post in Kinloch which contains a limited range of rescue equipment; but there is no formal mountain

rescue team on the island. Volunteers from the village will usually go out to provide help if there is concern about a missing walker. Formal emergency services can be summoned if a serious rescue is required.

On the Cuillin Ridge

CHAPTER 16

Making it Happen

FOR THE PAST 40 YEARS Rum has been in public ownership and has been managed as a National Nature Reserve; for all those years, 'primacy of nature' has been at the heart of decisions about land-use and management, and outright ownership has brought long-term continuity of management with few external constraints on policy.

But what of the next forty years? What of the next century? Scottish Natural Heritage has given a great deal of thought to the best way ahead for this 'flagship' National Nature Reserve; and in 1997 the Board of SNH endorsed a ringing **Statement of Intent** for the future of Rum.

The Statement of Intent

The Statement of Intent sets out SNH's vision for the island through the 21st century. It builds on Rum's first 40 years as a National Nature Reserve by reiterating that the primary object of management is to restore the island's fertility and productivity, as well as to increase its variety of landscape and wildlife. The key means of achieving these targets will be to re-establish the former mosaic of native woodland and scrub, while ensuring that red deer and goat numbers are kept at levels which provide an appropriate balance between grazing animals and the natural woody and shrubby vegetation:

> SNH's task on Rum is to provide a powerful demonstration of the practical gains – both to the environment and to the people of the western Highlands and beyond – which will accrue from the wise use and care of the natural resources of this fragile region. While safeguarding the quality of the existing natural heritage on Rum, SNH will accelerate the rate of restoration of the natural capital of the island – the native plant and animal communities which have been lost or degraded through centuries of human activity.

> As a result, we shall gain knowledge from the resultant increase in biological diversity and productivity, and we shall use this knowledge to give a wider understanding of natural processes, **and to show how greater human activity can be sustained.**

In making this commitment, SNH recognised that the key factor constraining the achievement of its vision is the current level of grazing. Red deer, ponies, Highland cattle and wild goats are all present, although the cattle in particular have a critical role in the island's natural biodiversity. The numbers of red deer (and, to a very much lesser extent, goats) severely constrain recovery of vegetation communities. SNH will make a substantial reduction in the numbers of red deer over the next ten years; however, it recognises the need to retain grazing in areas where this encourages, rather than hinders, the survival and spread of a wider range of plants.

The continued healing of the land will perforce be a slow process. It could take years for some elements of the island's ecosystem to recover naturally, especially where a species has disappeared from neighbouring areas; so where elements of the native fauna and flora of Rum have been lost as a result of human actions, SNH will undertake a measured programme of reintroductions. Even then, the past impact of peat-burning and the relentless effects of high rainfall will continue to limit the improvement in levels of productivity of the soil.

SNH remains committed to the concept of Rum as an 'outdoor laboratory', but will direct its own funds for future research towards achieving 'best management practice' for the natural heritage. SNH will continue to welcome research projects on aspects of the archaeology, history and natural history of Rum which support, and are consistent with, SNH's aims for the island. SNH is also committed to providing as many opportunities as possible for people not only to enjoy the natural heritage at its best but also to learn about, and feel they are involved in, major environmental issues.

The Statement of Intent provides the foundation for the ten-year framework of management which will operate from 1997. The Management Plan articulates the purpose of the Reserve, sets out a series of specific objectives, and identifies the means by which they will be achieved and reported. The major areas of work include:

- compiling and maintaining an inventory of natural heritage resources;
- researching Rum's special features and the Reserve's continuing programmes of habitat and species restoration;
- conserving and, where appropriate, enhancing natural and cultural heritage features;
- restoring native woodland and scrub as widely as possible (which will involve a substantial reduction in deer numbers), thereby providing a powerful demonstration of habitat restoration;
- protecting the features of interest from loss and damage;
- monitoring change in the features of interest;
- promoting the Reserve for education and training, which should highlight the island's potential as a demonstration site for sustainable land use;
- developing visitor facilities and services to facilitate informal recreation and enjoyment of the reserve;
- fostering a thriving community on Rum;

· ensuring that the Reserve is efficiently run;
· establishing new external funding and management arrangements for Kinloch Castle.

As was anticipated at the time of its acquisition, Rum has provided an unrivalled opportunity for research across a range of natural science disciplines. It is a place where many research themes come together: research on the ecology of individual species and habitats within the Highlands and Islands; on the conservation and management of native woodlands; on geology and processes which fashion the shape of our landscapes; and on the history of land-use in the Highlands. History and prehistory are of immense importance to nature conservation. There must be constant and fertile interchange of ideas between the disciplines of history, archaeology, geology and ecology: all are interdependent within the physical processes of land and landscape. A knowledge of the past, and of the cumulative effects of 9,000 years of human activity, is essential to a proper understanding of nature conservation in the human context.

Rum has also proved its worth for formal and informal education over the years. Several universities and colleges of further education regularly send geology students there as part of their courses. There are also ample opportunities for traditional field studies including botany, zoology and ecological relationships. Several informal educational groups make regular visits with extra-mural adult education classes in the early summer; there is potential for considerable expansion in this area. Rum is also used for the demonstration of environmental management, and many specialist groups have come to examine management practices and developments, especially those which concern the restoration of native woodland: indeed, there is a growing demand for environmental management courses based on the island.

These visits are of great use to Scottish Natural Heritage, too. Many of the groups contribute directly to our knowledge of the Reserve. Moray House College in Edinburgh has been visiting for 25 years, conducting an annual Common Bird Census – this has built up an invaluable record of the changing bird communities as the new woodland on Rum develops. In turn, Reserve staff support these groups with introductory lectures and occasional assistance in the field.

Kinloch Castle

When Rum was purchased for the nation in 1957, the extraordinary Edwardian monument of Kinloch Castle was included in the sale. This legacy of the early years of the 20th century remains largely unaltered since its Edwardian heyday (see CHAPTER 6). SNH believes that visitors to Rum should be encouraged to experience this flamboyant building and its contents; there is a daily guided tour conducted by the Castle manager.

Kinloch Castle is an ostentatious expression of one of the most recent periods of human history on Rum; but it has always been a millstone for the conservation agencies, whose expertise lies in nature conservation rather than in the preservation and utilisation of old buildings. In the early 1980s the Castle was a real problem for the NCC; it was being run as a hotel (but at a considerable loss), and it desperately needed expensive repairs. The porous Arran sandstone was drawing water into the Castle instead of excluding it, paintings and furniture were deteriorating in the very wet climate; walls and cornices were cracking. It was going to cost £500,000 to carry out the repairs and restoration work required; a further £500,000 was required to improve electricity generation for the island with a new hydro-scheme above the old dam in Coire Dubh. The National Trust for Scotland, with its curatorial expertise, was seen as the obvious custodian of the Castle to ensure its future in perpetuity, and there were protracted discussions between senior officials of the two bodies. However, the sum of money which would have been required to endow any transfer of ownership was very high (£2 million was mentioned); besides, the National Trust for Scotland, which already owned Fair Isle and St Kilda and was negotiating over Canna, was chary of accepting responsibility for yet another island. Despite good intentions on both sides, the negotiations came to nothing.

SNH has put a great deal of resources into maintaining the fabric of the Castle, but it will require considerable capital investment not simply to preserve the fabric of the Castle but also to enhance its attractions for visitors. The Castle, to be an asset rather than a burden, requires a great deal of inspired thinking. Thought is now being given to the possibility of setting up a separate Trust to run the Castle, perhaps financed by external sources such as the National Lottery. A partnership with the National Trust for Scotland, now the owners of the neighbouring island of Canna, could be worth exploring.

In July 1996, a number of enthusiasts, led by George Randall of Cumbria, formed a Kinloch Castle Friends Association; it now has about 20 members. George Randall has done a great deal of research into the story of the Castle, and Friends visit Rum occasionally to carry out minor but useful projects agreed by the Reserve manager. SNH welcomes such support and looks forward to harnessing the enthusiasm of the Friends to make a positive contribution to the future of the Castle.[1]

Whatever the management and funding arrangements, SNH is intent on the Castle being restored, with a view to sharing this national treasure with the public. SNH will always ensure that its management is fully in keeping with the pledge to Lady Bullough and the fulfilment of our vision for Rum.

---

[1] *Anyone interested in joining the Friends should contact George Randall at: Keepers Cottage, Cowgill, Dentdale, Sedbergh, Cumbria LA10 5RN. The annual subscription is £10.*

The cost

Rum doesn't come free; but it is helping to pay its own way. Scottish Natural Heritage spends just over £200,000 a year on Rum (both the National Nature Reserve and the Castle). In 1996/97 the gross expenditure was £323,000, and the gross income £109,500 – a net cost of £213,500. More than 90% of this total is spent on the NNR.[1]

Is it worth it? Is it a justifiable expenditure of public money? Is it, as the jargon goes, 'value for money?'

I have no doubt in my own mind that all the expenditure of time, effort and money on Rum over the years has been more than justified by the results: *si monumentum requiris, circumspice* – 'if you seek a monument, look around you'.

The island community

Scottish Natural Heritage has a responsibility to support a viable human community on Rum, and to have regard for its welfare. It maintains housing and related services and has built a Village Hall for community use.

Despite its small size, the community is vibrant. It enjoys a remarkable range of activities: the village store and the teashop are both run (independently) by the residents, while 'law and order' is maintained by a Special Constable and Receiver of Wrecks who happily has very little to do (he happens to be the Reserve manager, Martin Curry!). There is an Auxiliary Coastguard-in-Chief, with a team of six volunteers, and a Mountain Rescue post.

The school, with its full-time teacher provided by the Highland Council, provides small-scale employment for an auxiliary (a secretary) and a gardener, and there is a sub-Postmaster to deal with a delivery service paid for by the Royal Mail. There is also an official library service, and regular visits by the Church of Scotland minister from Arisaig provide religious services and support for the Sunday School.

The community has its own Association, which meets regularly to discuss local matters and organise a programme of social events such as ceilidhs, Christmas events, barbecues and so on.

Nonetheless, Scottish Natural Heritage is, at present, the primary employer on Rum, supporting one part-time and eight full-time posts. Currently there are a further eight dependants, as well as the school-teacher (Mrs Chrissie MacDougall from Mallaig) and two long-term researchers contracted to outside agencies. This makes a current population of only twenty people.

It means that the island relies almost entirely on subsidy from the

[1] *A breakdown of the figures shows that the National Nature Reserve cost £241,500 for staff, maintenance and project work; receipts from visitors, publications and sales of venison amounted to £44,000 – a net cost of £197,500. The Castle cost £81,500 for staff and maintenance work, and produced receipts of £65,500 from visitors – a net cost of £16,000.*

SNH waymarker at Kinloch

mainland – from Scottish Natural Heritage in Edinburgh; and that is not a healthy situation for any community. It needs to be able to sustain a community of people who 'belong' to Rum. It needs a dynamic community living and working in harmony with a dynamic environment. It needs to be given the opportunity to start to earn its own keep from that environment.

There has been talk of reviving the farming operation which the Bulloughs had promoted, but with a tenant farmer or tenant crofters who could work the land around Kinloch as small-holdings; or 'privatising' the fold of Highland cattle; or utilising the pony herd for pony-trekking; or encouraging small bed-and-breakfast facilities. SNH is currently exploring these and other options in close consultation with the community on Rum.

Maintaining a viable community on Rum is vital for the island's future. One of the critical problems is the education of its children. There is only a primary school, and the number of pupils can fall to perilously low levels at times. The absence of a secondary school means that families have to leave the island when children reach the age of 11 or 12 – or send their children away to board on the mainland.

Nor is there any provision for SNH staff members to stay on the island after they retire: the house goes with the job, and there would be nowhere for them to live. As a result, there are no grandparents on Rum, which means a demographically unbalanced community.

Scottish Natural Heritage is fully aware of all these problems, and is addressing them with determination. Already there are many ideas afoot for generating income from the island itself, and we are looking closely at the possibilities for helping the island to become socially and economically more self-supporting in the future.

The community of the Small Isles

A viable community on Rum is important in contributing to sustainable settlement in the Small Isles as a whole. Viewed from Arisaig, Ardnamurchan or the Isle of Skye, Rum is clearly an integral part of the Parish of the Small Isles along with its neighbours of Canna, Eigg and Muck. The interplay of land and sea in this corner of the Hebrides gives the area a very special quality. It is the sea which binds these islands together, for it is by the sea that they all share a common link.

SNH recognises the pivotal role which Rum can play in the community of the Small Isles. The islands' interdependence on a common transport link (through CalMac) is perhaps the most tangible aspect of this, and Rum will be a positive player in any proposals for a new slip for improved ferry access consistent with its role as a National Nature Reserve. The economic well-being of the Small Isles can only be enhanced by greater cohesion, and by taking the chance to share resources, skills (the doctor lives in Eigg, for instance, but is responsible for Rum as well) and commercial opportunities such as eco-tourism initiatives.

The Small Isles already have a Community Council where local social, domestic, economic and political issues are discussed. It has a voice in creating the Local Plan for the Lochaber district, of which it forms a part. And Rum plays its full part in the Small Isles occasions, by hosting the Small Isles Sports Gathering every fourth year. The roles of the four Small Isles – Rum (SNH), Canna (National Trust for Scotland), Eigg (community ownership) and the Muck estate – are all cognate; a grand heritage plan for the Small Isles should be an objective for the future.

In pursuing the vision for the future, SNH believes that Rum can offer powerful lessons for the wider West Highlands of Scotland where the over-exploitation of natural resources over many centuries has seriously depleted the carrying capacity of the land. SNH's vision is of an island which, a century from now, is not just biologically more diverse and productive but is also more economically dynamic and ecologically sustainable.

Appendix A An island chronology

3 billion years ago	Underlying rocks formed
800 million years	Tropical flood-plain
60 million years	Volcanic period
2 million years	Ice Ages start
9-8,000 BC	Ice Ages end
7,000 BC	Mesolithic settlers at Kinloch
3,000 BC	Neolithic Age
1,000 NC	Bronze Age cairns
400 BC	Iron Age: promontory forts built on Rum
7th century AD	St Beccán of Rum
9th century	Viking Age
1499	Macleans of Coll
1795	Population peak (443)
1826-28	Rum Clearances
1845	Rum bought by the Marquis of Salisbury
1863	Rum grazings let to Capt. Campbell of Ballinaby
1870	Rum bought by Farquhar Campbell of Aros
1879	Shooting rights let to John Bullough
1888	Rum bought by John Bullough for £35,000
1890	Start of policy woodland plantations
1891	Rum inherited by George Bullough
1897-1900	Kinloch Castle built
1901	George Bullough knighted
1903	Bullough marries Monica Charrington (de la Pasture)
1939	Death of Sir George Bullough
1957	Rum bought by the Nature Conservancy: National Nature Reserve declared
1967	Death of Lady Monica Bullough
1973	Nature Conservancy Council (NCC)
1975	White-tailed (sea) eagle reintroductions start
1992	Rum 'inherited' by Scottish Natural Heritage
1997	'Millionth tree' planted on Rum

Appendix B

Designations

Rum occupies a distinctive position among Britain's NNRs: it is one of the largest (10,700 ha), and many aspects of its diverse geology, terrain and associated wildlife are unique or among the best examples of their kind.

The island has also gained international recognition: it was designated a **Biosphere Reserve** by UNESCO in 1976. In 1977 it was identified as internationally important for its coastland, and nationally important for upland grasslands and wet heaths, in *A Nature Conservation Review*, with an additional commendation for its significant peatland interest.

In 1982, under the EU Wild Birds Directive, it was designated a **Special Protection Area** (SPA) for its Manx shearwaters. In 1987 it was re-notified as a **Site of Special Scientific Interest** (SSSI) by the Nature Conservation Council. In 1997, under the EU Habitats Directive, it became a candidate **Special Area of Conservation** (SAC) .

In 1987, seven Geological Conservation Review sites were recognised by the NCC: six for their Tertiary igneous interest, and one for the assemblage of periglacial landforms.

The island also forms a central component of the Small Isles **National Scenic Area** (NSA), designated in 1978 by the Countryside Commission for Scotland.

Rum has a remarkable legacy of historic sites and monuments (see CHAPTER 1). Almost 200 archaeological sites and monuments have been identified. The first ancient monument was scheduled in 1968. The first four buildings/structures were listed in 1971; another was listed in 1982, and two more in 1985. Another 16 ancient monuments were scheduled by Historic Scotland in 1996.

Acknowledgements and Sources

CHAPTER 1 In the Beginning.

Rum, in the 'Landscape Fashioned by Geology' series, by Rob Threadgould (forthcoming); 'Rum: an inactive volcano with an active role to play', by Rob Threadgould, in *Scotland's Natural Heritage* (SNH, Summer 1997); 'Rum-bustious! Island's violent past revealed', by Michael Cheadle, Martin Curry, C H Emeleus and Robert Hunter, in *Earth Heritage Magazine* (forthcoming); *Landforms and the Landscape: the Isle of Rum,* by John Gordon (unpublished draft); 'The Small Isles', in *British Tertiary Volcanic Province,* by C H Emeleus & M C Gyopari (JNCC GCR, Vol 4, 1992); 'The Tertiary Volcanic Province', by C H Emeleus, in *The Geology of Scotland,* ed G Craig (Oliver & Boyd, 1988); 'The Rhum Volcano', by C H Emeleus, in *Rum: The Natural History of an Island* (EUP 1987); *Six Inner Hebrides,* by Noel Banks (David & Charles, 1977); *The Hebrides: A Mosaic of Islands,* by J M Boyd & I L Boyd (Birlinn Press, 1996); 'Rhum – The Research Island', in *A Mosaic of Islands,* by Kenneth Williamson and Morton Boyd (Oliver and Boyd, 1963).
With help from Roger Crofts, John Gordon, Alan McKirdy and Rob Threadgould.

CHAPTER 2 The Coming of Man

Scotland's First Settlers, by Caroline Wickham-Jones (Batsford/Historic Scotland, 1994); 'Revealing Rum's Past', by Caroline Wickham-Jones and Dave Pollok (*Scots Magazine,* May 1986); *The Archaeological Sites and Monuments of Scotland: No 20, Rhum* (RCAHMS, 1983); *Portrait of Rum,* by John Walters (unpublished); *The Isle of Rum,* by John A Love (booklet, 1983).
With help from Ian Fisher, RCAHMS, and Caroline Wickham-Jones.

CHAPTER 3 Lords of the Isle

The Isle of Rum – A Short History, by John A Love, 1983; 'Rhum's Human History', in *Rhum: The Natural History of an Island,* by John Love (EUP 1987); *Report on the Hebrides of 1764 and 1771,* by John Walker (ed. M M Mackay, Edinburgh 1980); *A Description of the Western Isles of Scotland,* by Martin Martin (1703); *Life and remains of Edward Daniel Clarke DD,* 1834; *Remarks on the Evils at present Affecting the Highlands and Islands of Scotland,* by Allan Fullerton and Charles R Baird (1838); *The Highlands and Western Islands of Scotland,* by John MacCulloch (1824); *A tour in Scotland and voyage to the Hebrides,* by Thomas Pennant (1772); *The Cruise of the Betsey,* by Hugh Miller (1879); *The Limping Pilgrim, on his Wanderings,* by Edwin Waugh (1883); *Hakon the Old – Hakon Who?* by Magnus Magnusson (Largs, 1982); *Portrait of Rum,* by John Walters (unpublished); 'Shielings of the Isle of Rum', by John A Love, in *Scottish Studies* (Vol 25, 1982); *Collins Encyclopaedia of Scotland,* ed J & J Keay (Harper Collins, 1994)
With help from Chris Smout.

CHAPTER 4 A Sporting Estate

The Isle of Rum – A Short History, by John A Love, 1983; 'Rhum's Human History', in *Rhum: The Natural History of an Island,* by John Love (EUP 1987); *The Limping Pilgrim, on his Wanderings,* by Edwin Waugh (1883); *Portrait of Rum,* by John Walters (unpublished); 'Shielings of the Isle of Rum', by John A Love, in *Scottish Studies* (Vol 25, 1982).
With help from John Love.

CHAPTER 5 Enter the Bulloughs

Accrington Captains of Industry, by R S Crossley (Accrington, 1930); obituary of John Bullough, *Accrington Observer and Times*, February 28, 1891; *Industrial Heritage: A Guide to the Industrial Archaeology of Accrington*, by Mike Rothwell (1978); *The Textile Industry*, by W English (Industrial Archaeology Series, Longman, 1969); *The Cotton Masters 1830-1860*, by Anthony Howe (Oxford Historical Monographs, Clarendon Press, 1984); *The Lancashire Cotton Industry: A History Since 1700*, ed by Mary B Case (Lancashire County Books, 1996); 'Accrington's Rhum Connection', by J V Thomlinson (in *The Journal of the Accrington Naturalists' and Antiquarians' Society*, No 12, 1982/83); *The Limping Pilgrim, on his Wanderings*, by Edwin Waugh (1883)
With help from George Randall (Kinloch Castle Friends Association), Martin Wyatt, Norma Monks (Divisional Librarian, Lancashire County Library) and Catherine Duckworth (Accrington Local Studies Library).

CHAPTER 6 Kinloch Castle

SOURCES: 'How Strange a Cycle', by John Love (in *Scotland's Natural Heritage*, 1997); presentation by Clive Hollingworth, Hotel Manager at Kinloch Castle, during the Board tour, April 1997; 'Kinloch Castle, Isle of Rhum: a Property of the Nature Conservancy Council' (in two parts), by Clive Aslet (*Country Life*, August 9 & 16, 1984); 'Rhum and Kinloch Castle', by John Betjeman (*Scotland's Magazine*, December 1959); *Bare Feet and Tackety Boots*, by Archie Cameron (Luath Press, 1988); 'Kinloch Castle', by Tim Willis and Lucinda Lambton *(World of Interiors*, December 1985); *A Magical Place*, by Tim Willis (in *Scottish Field*, December 1985); *A to Z of Britain*, by Lucinda Lambton (Harper Collins, 1996); *Napoleon's Family*, by Desmond Seward (Weidenfeld & Nicholson, 1986); 'A Talent Reassessed' [on Byron Cooper], by Maurice Ridgway (in *Watercolours*, Summer 1993); unpublished research notes by George W Randall; (unsigned) two-part feature in *The Scots Magazine* (July & August 1978).
With help from Martin Curry, Clive Hollingworth and George Randall; family anecdotes from Lord Lambton, Lucy Lambton, and Angus Mackenzie-Charrington; and help from Oliver Everett (Royal Library, Windsor Castle) and Diana Lay (The Bass Museum, Burton upon Trent).

CHAPTER 7 A National Nature Reserve

'Management Plan 1960-64' (Nature Conservancy, 1959: published in the first issue of the *Journal of Applied Ecology* in 1964); *NNR Policy Review: Foundation Document* (March 1996); John Walters, *Portrait of Rum* (unpublished draft, pp 44-45); *Minute of Agreement* between Dame Monica Lilly Bullough and the Nature Conservancy, 1957; *Disposition* by the Trustees of Sir George Bullough in favour of the Nature Conservancy, 1957; 'Rum Management Plan' (SNH, 1997).
With help from John Arbuthnott, John Morton Boyd, Martin Curry, Peter Mackay, Max Nicholson, and Peter and Jessie Wormell.

CHAPTER 8 Regeneration of the Woodlands

'The Regeneration of Rum', by Magnus Magnusson, in *Scotland's Natural Heritage* (Summer 1997); 'Botany, Woodland and Forestry', by M E Ball, in *Rhum: The Natural History of an Island* (EUP 1987); *The Hebrides*, Vol. 3, by J M Boyd and I L Boyd (1996); *A Mosaic of Islands*, by Kenneth Williamson and Morton Boyd (Oliver and Boyd, 1963); *Portrait of Rum*, by John Walters (unpublished).
With help from John Morton Boyd, Michael B Usher and Peter Wormell.

CHAPTER 9 Rum in Flower

'Botany, Woodland and Forestry', by M E Ball, in *Rhum: the Natural History of an Island* (EUP 1987); *Portrait of Rum*, by John Walters (unpublished); *Collins Guide to Scottish Wild Flowers*, by Michael Scott (1996); 'Mountain Plants of the Small Isles' by Michael Scott, in *Discover Scotland* (Part 40, 1990); *The Encyclopaedia of Medicinal Plants*, by Andrew Chevallier (Dorling Kindersley, 1996); SNH Species Action Programme, 1996.
With help from Martin Ball and Michael Scott; additional help from John Morton Boyd, Chris Sydes, Anne Taylor and Michael B Usher.

CHAPTER 10 Birdlife

Shearwaters: 'The Manx Shearwaters of Rhum', by Peter Wormell (*Scottish Birds*, 1976, Vol. 9, pp 103-118); *The Manx Shearwater*, by Michael Brooke (Poyser, 1990); 'The ecology of the Manx Shearwater *Puffinus puffinus* on Rhum, West Scotland', by K R Thompson (PhD thesis, University of Glasgow, 1987); Schools Hebridean Society Annual Reports (intermittently 1963-1981); 'The Birds of Rhum', by John Love and Peter Wormell, in *Rhum: The Natural History of an Island* (EUP, 1987); 'The Shearwaters of Rum' in *An Island Here and There*, by Alasdair Alpin MacGregor (Kingsmead Press, 1972); 'Wild Island Nightlife Attracts High Flyers', by John Walters, in *Scotland's Natural Heritage* (SNH, Summer 1997); *Book of British Birds* (Reader's Digest, 1969).
Sea eagles: *Sea Eagles*, by Greg Mudge, Kevin Duffy, Kate Thompson and John Love (Scottish Natural Heritage 1996); 'Long-term viability of the re-introduced population of the White-tailed eagle *Haliaeetus albicilla* in Scotland', by R E Green, M W Pienkowski and J A Love (*Journal of Applied Ecology*, 1996, Vol. 33, pp 357-68); 'The Birds of Rhum', by John Love and Peter Wormell, in *Rhum: The Natural History of an Island* (EUP, 1987); *The sea eagle* (NCC, 1985); *Sea eagle project*, Newsletters, 1993-1996; with additional help from Andy Douse, John Love and John Walters.
General: 'The Birds of Rhum', by J A Love and P Wormell, in *Rhum: The Natural History of an Island* (EUP, 1987); *Isle of Rum – Nature Trails* (SNH 1993); *The Hebrides*, Vol. 3, by J M Boyd and I L Boyd (Birlinn Press, 1996).
With help from Des Thompson; additional help from John Morton Boyd, Andy Douse, John Love, Michael B Usher and John Walters.

CHAPTER 11 Red Deer on Rum

'Global recognition for red deer', by Peter Tilbrook, in *Scotland's Natural Heritage* (Summer 1997); 'Manipulation of red deer density on Rum', by Tim Clutton-Brock (SNH Information and Advisory Note, 1997); *Red Deer in the Highlands*, by T H Clutton-Brock and S D Albon (BSP Professional Books, Oxford, 1984); *Red Deer and the Natural Heritage* (SNH Policy Paper, 1994); 'Trial and Error in the Highlands', by T H Clutton-Brock and S D Albon, in *Nature* (358: 11-12, 1982); 'Red Deer', by T H Clutton-Brock and F E Guinness, in *Rhum: the Natural History of an Island* (EUP, 1987); John Walters, *Portrait of Rum* (unpublished, 1997); 'Deer Traps on the Isle of Rum', by John A Love, in *Deer*, 5 (1980); 'Rhum Returns to Nature', by Michael Jenner, in *The Geographical Magazine Travel Guide* (February 1986).
With help from Steve Albon, Tim Clutton-Brock, Pat Lowe and Brian Staines, and from Helen Armstrong, Des Thompson and Michael B Usher (SNH).

CHAPTER 12 Ponies, Highland Cattle, Goats and Other Mammals

Ponies: *A tour in Scotland and voyage to the Hebrides,* by Thomas Pennant (1772); *A Journey to the Western Isles of Scotland*, by Dr Johnson (1775); *Old Statistical Account* (1796); *Bare Feet and Tackety Boots*, by Archie Cameron (Luath Press, 1988); *Portrait of*

Rum, by John Walters (unpublished, 1997); Martin Curry, *The Ponies of Rum* (article in *Riders' Journal*, 1993); 'Rhum and Rhum Ponies', by Margaret Mason (March 1, 1982); 'Ponies, Cattle and Goats' in *Rhum: the Natural History of an Island* (EUP 1987).
Highland cattle: *General View of the Agriculture of the Hebrides*, by James Macdonald (1811); 'Highland Cattle on the Hebridean island of Rum', by C. J. Eatough, in *Proceedings of the First International Gathering of Highland Cattle Breeders* (1995); Keynote Speech, by Magnus Magnusson (*ibid*).
Goats: *Report on the Hebrides of 1764 and 1771*, by John Walker; *Portrait of Rum*, by John Walters (unpublished); *Rhum: the Natural History of an Island* (1987): *An Island Here and There*, by Alistair Alpin MacGregor (1972); *A Mosaic of Islands*, by Kenneth Williams (1963); 'Feral goats on Rhum 1960-78', by I. L Boyd (in *Journal of Zoology*).
With help from John Morton Boyd, Martin Curry, Chris Etough and Michael B Usher.

CHAPTER 13 Insect Life
'Invertebrates of Rhum', by Peter Wormell, in *Rhum: The Natural History of an Island* (EUP, 1987); *Portrait of Rum*, by John Walters (unpublished draft, 1997); *The Entomology of the Isle of Rhum National Nature Reserve*, edited by P Wormell (*Biological Journal of the Linnean Society*, 1982); Rum NNR Wildlife Reports (1992-93, 1994); David Phillips, 'Invertebrates of Rum' (incomplete catalogue); 'A new species of bird flea from the Manx shearwater in Scotland', by M B Usher (*Entomologist's Gazette*, Vol 19, 1967); 'Some spiders and harvestmen from Rhum, Scotland', by M B Usher (The British Spider Study Group, Bulletin No 39, July 1968).
With help from Peter Wormell and Michael B Usher.

CHAPTER 14 The Surrounding Seas
Memorandum by Ben Leyshon, SNH, on the Rum Management Plan (April 1997); 'Life in the Sea' and 'The Sea Shore', in *The Hebrides: A Natural Tapestry*, by J M and I L Boyd (Birlinn Press, 1996): 'The Seas of Plenty', by John Hambrey (in *The Nature of Scotland*, Canongate, 1991).
With help from John Baxter, John Morton Boyd, Ben Leyshon and Michael B Usher.

CHAPTER 15 Accommodating Visitors
Rum Nature Reserve leaflets; 'Nature Trails on Rum' (SNH); 'The Cuillin of Rum', by Mark Richards, in *The Climber and Rambler* (December 1978); *The Island of Rhum: a Guide for walkers, climbers and visitors*, by Hamish M Brown (Cicerone Press, 1995).
With help from Martin Curry, Alastair M Dunnett, Roddy Fairley, Peter Mackay and Anne Taylor.

CHAPTER 16 Making it Happen
'Statement of Intent' (SNH 1997); Rum Management Plan (SNH, 1997).
With help from John Morton Boyd, Roger Crofts, Roddy Fairley, Peter Mackay, John Walters and Jeff Watson.

ACKNOWLEDGEMENTS AND SOURCES

Picture, Illustration and Map Acknowledgements

Thanks are due to many people for permission to reproduce photographs and drawings: Lorne Gill (SNH Design & Publications) for the cover photograph of Rum, and for photographs on pp 19, 42; Wendy Price (cartographer) for the charts on pp 1, 3, 110 and at the front of the book; Iain Sarjeant, for all the line drawings; Scottish Natural Heritage, for the photographs on pp 18, 25, 38, 47, 49, 57; The British Library, for the copy of *The Times* advertisement in 1886 p 26; Lancashire County Library: Accrington Local Studies Library, for photographs of James, John and George Bullough pp 27, 30, 33, and the Globe Works p28; George Randall (Friends of Kinloch Castle Association), for photographs of the Castle and contents pp 39, 41, 43, 44, 45, 50, and others pp 34, 36; Martin Howells, for his sketch of the Castle conservatory p 37; Angus Mackenzie-Charrington, for permission to reproduce the painting of Monica Charrington p 40 and Roger Crofts (SNH Chief Executive) for photographs on pp 62, 119.

Index

Bare Feet & TacketyBoots

A boyhood on the island of Rhum

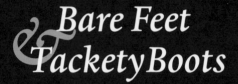

ARCHIE CAMERON

The authentic breath of the pawky,
country-wise estate employee.'
THE OBSERVER

Some other books published by **LUATH** PRESS

BIOGRAPHY

Bare Feet and Tackety Boots

Archie Cameron

ISBN 0 946487 17 0 PBK £7.95

The island of Rum before the First World War was the playground of its rich absentee landowner. A survivor of life a century gone tells his story. Factors and schoolmasters, midges and poaching, deer, ducks and MacBrayne's steamers: here social history and personal anecdote create a record of a way of life gone not long ago but already almost forgotten. This is the story the gentry couldn't tell.

'This book is an important piece of social history, for it gives an insight into how the other half lived in an era the likes of which will never be seen again'
FORTHRIGHT MAGAZINE

'The authentic breath of the pawky, country-wise estate employee.'
THE OBSERVER

'Well observed and detailed account of island life in the early years of this century'
THE SCOTS MAGAZINE

'A very good read with the capacity to make the reader chuckle. A very talented writer.'
STORNOWAY GAZETTE

On the Trail of Robert Service

Wallace Lockhart

ISBN 0 946487 24 3 PBK £5.95

Known worldwide for his verses 'The Shooting of Dan McGrew' and 'The Cremation of Sam McGee', Service has woven his spell for Boy Scouts and learned professors alike. He chronicled the story of the Klondike Gold Rush, wandered the United States and Canada, Tahiti and Russia to become the bigger-than-life Bard of the Yukon. Whether you love or hate him, you can't ignore this cult figure. The book is a must for those who haven't yet met Robert Service.

'The story of a man who claimed that he wrote verse for those who wouldn't be seen dead reading poetry... this enthralling biography will delight Service lovers in both the Old World and the New.'
SCOTS INDEPENDENT

Come Dungeons Dark

John Taylor Caldwell

ISBN 0 946487 19 7 PBK £6.95

Glasgow anarchist Guy Aldred died with 10p in his pocket in 1963 claiming there was better company in Barlinnie Prison than in the Corridors of Power. 'The Red Scourge' is remembered here by one who worked with him and spent 27 years as part of his turbulent household, sparring with Lenin, Sylvia Pankhurst and others as he struggled for freedom for his beloved fellow-man.

'The welcome and long-awaited biography of... one of this country's most prolific radical propagandists... Crank or visionary?... whatever the verdict, the Glasgow anarchist has finally been given a fitting memorial.'
THE SCOTSMAN

Seven Steps in the Dark

Bob Smith

ISBN 0 946487 21 9 PBK £8.95

'The story of his 45 years working at the faces of seven of Scotland's mines... full of dignity and humanity... unrivalled comradeship... a vivid picture of mining life with all its heartbreaks and laughs.'
SCOTTISH MINER

Bob Smith went into the pit when he was fourteen years old to work with his father. They toiled in a low seam, just a few inches high, lying in the coal dust and mud, getting the coal out with pick and shovel. This is his story, but it is also the story of the last forty years of Scottish coalmining. A staunch Trades Unionist, one of those once described as "the enemy within", his life shows that in fact he has been dedicated utterly to the betterment of his fellow human beings.

LUATH GUIDES TO SCOTLAND

'Gentlemen, We have just returned from a six week stay in Scotland. I am convinced that Tom Atkinson is the best guidebook author I have ever read, about any place, any time.'
Edward Taylor, LOS ANGELES

These guides are not your traditional where-to-stay and what-to-eat books. They are companions in the rucksack or car seat, providing the discerning traveller with a blend of fiery opinion and moving description. Here you will find *'that curious pastiche of myths and legend and history that the Scots use to describe their heritage... what battle happened in which glen between which clans; where the Picts sacrificed bulls as recently as the 17th century... A lively counterpoint to the more standard, detached guidebook... Intriguing.'*
THE WASHINGTON POST

These are perfect guides for the discerning visitor or resident to keep close by for reading again and again, written by authors who invite you to share their intimate knowledge and love of the areas covered.

South West Scotland
Tom Atkinson
ISBN 0 946487 04 9 PBK £4.95
This descriptive guide to the magical country of Robert Burns covers Kyle, Carrick, Galloway, Dumfries-shire, Kirkcudbrightshire and Wigtownshire. Hills, unknown moors and unspoiled beaches grace a land steeped in history and legend and portrayed with affection and deep delight.
An essential book for the visitor who

yearns to feel at home in this land of peace and grandeur.

The Lonely Lands
Tom Atkinson
ISBN 0 946487 10 3 PBK £4.95
A guide to Inveraray, Glencoe, Loch Awe, Loch Lomond, Cowal, the Kyles of Bute and all of central Argyll written with insight, sympathy and loving detail. Once Atkinson has taken you there, these lands can never feel lonely. 'I have sought to make the complex simple, the beautiful accessible and the strange familiar,' he writes, and indeed he brings to the land a knowledge and affection only accessible to someone with intimate knowledge of the area.
A must for travellers and natives who want to delve beneath the surface.

'Highly personal and somewhat quirky... steeped in the lore of Scotland.'
THE WASHINGTON POST

The Empty Lands
Tom Atkinson
ISBN 0 946487 13 8 PBK £4.95
The Highlands of Scotland from Ullapool to Bettyhill and Bonar Bridge to John O'Groats are landscapes of myth and legend, 'empty of people, but of nothing else that brings delight to any tired soul,' writes Atkinson. This highly personal guide describes Highland history and landscape with love, compassion and above all sheer magic.
Essential reading for anyone who has dreamed of the Highlands.

Roads to the Isles
Tom Atkinson
ISBN 0 946487 01 4 PBK £4.95
Ardnamurchan, Morvern, Morar, Moidart and the west coast to Ullapool are included in this guide to the Far West and Far North of Scotland. An unspoiled land of mountains, lochs and silver sands is brought to the walker's toe-tips (and to the reader's fingertips) in this stark, serene and evocative account of town,

country and legend.

For any visitor to this Highland wonderland, Queen Victoria's favourite place on earth.

Highways and Byways in Mull and Iona

Peter Macnab

ISBN 0 946487 16 2 PBK £4.25

'The Isle of Mull is of Isles the fairest, Of ocean's gems 'tis the first and rarest.' So a local poet described it a hundred years ago, and this recently revised guide to Mull and sacred Iona, the most accessible islands of the Inner Hebrides, takes the reader on a delightful tour of these rare ocean gems, travelling with a native whose unparalleled knowledge and deep feeling for the area unlock the byways of the islands in all their natural beauty.

The Speyside Holiday Guide

Ernest Cross

ISBN 0 946487 27 8 PBK £4.95

Toothache in Tomintoul? Golf in Garmouth? Whatever your questions, Ernest Cross has the answers in this witty and knowledgeable guide to Speyside, one of Scotland's most popular holiday centres. A must for visitors and residents alike - there are still secrets to be discovered here!

WALK WITH LUATH

Mountain Days & Bothy Nights

Dave Brown and Ian Mitchell

ISBN 0 946487 15 4 PBK £7.50

Acknowledged as a classic of mountain writing still in demand ten years after its first publication, this book takes you into the bothies, howffs and dosses on the Scottish hills. Fishgut Mac, Desperate Dan and Stumpy the Big Yin stalk hill and public house, evading gamekeepers and Royalty with a camaraderie which was the trademark of Scots hillwalking in the early days.

'The fun element comes through... how innocent the social polemic seems in our nastier world of today... the book for the rucksack this year.'
Hamish Brown, SCOTTISH MOUNTAINEERING CLUB JOURNAL

'The doings, sayings, incongruities and idiosyncrasies of the denizens of the bothy underworld... described in an easy philosophical style... an authentic word picture of this part of the climbing scene in latter-day Scotland, which, like any good picture, will increase in charm over the years.'
Iain Smart, SCOTTISH MOUNTAINEERING CLUB JOURNAL

'The ideal book for nostalgic hillwalkers of the 60s, even just the armchair and public house variety... humorous, entertaining, informative, written by two men with obvious expertise, knowledge and love of their subject.'
SCOTS INDEPENDENT

'Fifty years have made no difference. Your crowd is the one I used to know... [This] must be the only complete dossers' guide ever put together.'
Alistair Borthwick, author of the immortal *Always a Little Further.*

The Joy of Hillwalking

Ralph Storer

ISBN 0 946487 28 6 PBK £6.95

Apart, perhaps, from the joy of sex, the joy of hillwalking brings more pleasure to more people than any other form of human activity.

'Alps, America, Scandinavia, you name it – Storer's been there, so why the hell shouldn't he bring all these various and varied places into his observations... [He] even admits to losing his virginity after a day on the Aggy Ridge... Well worth its place alongside Storer's earlier works.'
TAC

LUATH WALKING GUIDES

The highly respected and continually updated guides to the Cairngorms.

'Particularly good on local wildlife and how to see it'
THE COUNTRYMAN

Walks in the Cairngorms

Ernest Cross
ISBN 0 946487 09 X PBK £3.95
This selection of walks celebrates the rare birds, animals, plants and geological wonders of a region often believed difficult to penetrate on foot. Nothing is difficult with this guide in your pocket, as Cross gives a choice for every walker, and includes valuable tips on mountain safety and weather advice.
Ideal for walkers of all ages and skiers waiting for snowier skies.

Short Walks in the Cairngorms

Ernest Cross
ISBN 0 946487 23 5 PBK £3.95
Cross wrote this volume after overhearing a walker remark that there were no short walks for lazy ramblers in the Cairngorm region. Here is the answer: rambles through scenic woods with a welcoming pub at the end, birdwatching hints, glacier holes, or for the fit and ambitious, scrambles up hills to admire vistas of glorious scenery. Wildlife in the Cairngorms is unequalled elsewhere in Britain, and here it is brought to the binoculars of any walker who treads quietly and with respect.

HUMOUR/HISTORY

Revolting Scotland

Jeff Fallow
ISBN 0 946487 23 1 PBK £5.95
No Heiland Flings, tartan tams and kilty dolls in this witty and cutting cartoon history of bonnie Scotland frae the Ice Age tae Maggie Thatcher.

'An ideal gift for all Scottish teenagers.'
SCOTS INDEPENDENT

'The quality of the drawing [is] surely inspired by Japanese cartoonist Keiji Nakazawa whose books powerfully encapsulated the horror of Hiroshima… refreshing to see a strong new medium like this.'
CHAPMAN

SOCIAL HISTORY

The Crofting Years

Francis Thompson
ISBN 0 946487 06 5 PBK £5.95
Crofting is much more than a way of life. It is a storehouse of cultural, linguistic and moral values which holds together a scattered and struggling rural population. This book fills a blank in the written history of crofting over the last two centuries. Bloody conflicts and gunboat diplomacy, treachery, compassion, music and story: all figure in this mine of information on crofting in the Highlands and Islands of Scotland.

'I would recommend this book to all who are interested in the past, but even more so to those who are interested in the future survival of our way of life and culture'
STORNOWAY GAZETTE

'A cleverly planned book… the story told in simple words which compel attention… [by] a Gaelic speaking Lewisman with specialised knowledge of the crofting community.'
BOOKS IN SCOTLAND

'The book is a mine of information on many aspects of the past, among them the homes, the food, the music and the medicine of our crofting forebears.'
John M Macmillan, erstwhile CROFTERS COMMISSIONER FOR LEWIS AND HARRIS

'This fascinating book is recommended to anyone who has the interests of our language and culture at heart.'
Donnie Maclean, DIRECTOR OF AN COMUNN GAIDHEALACH, WESTERN ISLES

'Unlike many books on the subject,

Crofting Years combines a radical politi-
cal approach to Scottish crofting experi-
ence with a ruthless realism which while
recognising the full tragedy and difficulty
of his subject never descends to sentimen-
tality or nostalgia'
CHAPMAN

MUSIC AND DANCE

Highland Balls and Village Halls

Wallace Lockhart

ISBN 0 946487 12 X   PBK   £6.95

Acknowledged as a classic in Scottish
dancing circles throughout the world.
Anecdotes, Scottish history, dress and
dance steps are all included in this
'delightful little book, full of interest...
both a personal account and an under-
standing look at the making of tradi-
tions.'
NEW ZEALAND SCOTTISH COUNTRY
DANCES MAGAZINE

'A delightful survey of Scottish dancing
and custom. Informative, concise and
opinionated, it guides the reader across
the history and geography of country
dance and ends by detailing the 12 dances
every Scot should know – the most
famous being the Eightsome Reel, "the
greatest longest, rowdiest, most diaboli-
cally executed of all the Scottish country
dances".'
THE HERALD

'A pot-pourri of every facet of Scottish
country dancing. It will bring back mem-
ories of petronella turns and poussettes
and make you eager to take part in a
Broun's reel or a dashing white
sergeant!'
DUNDEE COURIER AND ADVERTISER

'An excellent an very readable insight
into the traditions and customs of
Scottish country dancing. The author
takes us on a tour from his own early
days jigging in the village hall to the
characters and traditions that have made
our own brand of dance popular through-
out the world.'
SUNDAY POST

POETRY

The Jolly Beggars or 'Love and Liberty'

Robert Burns

ISBN 0 946487 02 2   HB   8.00

Forgotten by the Bard himself, the redis-
covery of this manuscript caused storms
of acclaim at the turn of the 19th
century. Yet it is hardly known today. It
was set to music to form the only canta-
ta ever written by Burns. SIR WALTER
SCOTT wrote: 'Laid in the very lowest
department of low life, the actors being
a set of strolling vagrants... extravagant
glee and outrageous frolic... not, perhaps, to be paralleled in the English language.' This edition is printed in Burns'
own handwriting with an informative
introduction by Tom Atkinson.

'The combination of facsimile, lively John
Hampson graphics and provocative
comment on the text makes for enjoy-
able reading.'
THE SCOTSMAN

Poems to be Read Aloud

selected and introduced by Tom Atkinson

ISBN 0 946487 00 6   PBK   £5.00

This personal collection of doggerel and
verse ranging from the tear-jerking
'Green Eye of the Yellow God' to the
rarely-printed bawdy 'Eskimo Nell' has a
lively cult following. Much borrowed
and rarely returned, this is a book for
reading aloud in very good company,
preferably after a dram or twa. You are
guaranteed a warm welcome if you
arrive at a gathering with this little volume in your pocket.

'The essence is the audience.'
Tom Atkinson

FOLKLORE

The Supernatural Highlands

Francis Thompson

ISBN 0 946487 31 6 PBK £8.99

An authoritative exploration of the oth-
erworld of the Highlander, happenings
and beings hitherto thought to be out-
with the ordinary forces of nature. A
simple introduction to the way of life of
rural Highland and Island communities,
this new edition weaves a path through
second sight, the evil eye, witchcraft,
ghosts, fairies and other supernatural
beings, offering new sight-lines on areas
of belief once dismissed as folklore and
superstition.

Luath Press Limited

committed to publishing well written books worth reading

LUATH PRESS takes its name from Robert Burns, whose little collie
Luath (*Gael.,* swift or nimble) tripped up Jean Armour at a wedding and
gave him the chance to speak to the woman who was to be his wife and
the abiding love of his life. Burns called one of *The Twa Dogs* Luath after
Cuchullin's hunting dog in Ossian's Fingal. Luath Press grew up in the
heart of Burns country, and now resides a few steps up the road from
Burns' first lodgings in Edinburgh's Royal Mile.
Luath offers you distinctive writing with a hint of unexpected pleasures.

Most UK bookshops either carry our books in stock or can order them for
you. To order direct from us, please send a £sterling cheque, postal order,
international money order or your credit card details (number, address of
cardholder and expiry date) to us at the address below. Please add post
and packing as follows: UK – £1.00 per delivery address; overseas surface
mail – £2.50 per delivery address; overseas airmail – £3.50 for the first book
to each delivery address, plus £1.00 for each additional book by airmail to
the same address. If your order is a gift, we will happily enclose your card
or message at no extra charge.

Luath Press Limited
543/2 Castlehill
The Royal Mile
Edinburgh EH1 2ND
Telephone: 0131 225 4326
Fax: 0131 225 4324
email: gavin.macdougall@luath.co.uk
Website: www.luath.co.uk